The History and I
of Falconry

The History and Practice of Falconry

ALLAN OSWALD

formerly falconer to the Earl of Bradford at Weston Park, Shropshire and Viscount Massereene and Ferrard of Chilham Castle, Kent. Now resident falconer at Leighton Hall, Carnforth, Lancashire.

JERSEY
NEVILLE SPEARMAN

First published in Great Britain in 1982 by
Neville Spearman (Jersey) Limited
PO Box 75, Normandy House, St. Helier, Jersey
Channel Islands

Distributed by Neville Spearman Limited
The Priory Gate, Friars Street
Sudbury, Suffolk

ISBN 0 85978 045 7 (case)
ISBN 0 85978 050 3 (paper)

Typeset in 11 on 12 point Garamond
Printed by Hillman Printers Ltd
Frome, Somerset

Contents

for Simon

whose early childhood was, to a large
extent governed by the need of 'the birds'
and in whose generation's hands the future
of falconry with all its traditions and
history lies.

and Pegasus

who has been giving public displays ever
since he came to this country from France
when he was five years old. For about
25 years he's entertained and educated
giving great pleasure to countless thousands
of spectators and, judging from his attitude
both enjoyed and been proud to do it. Truly
an eagle in a million.

Introduction

I am often asked why or when I became interested in falconry. The honest answer is that I just don't know. I think it just happened. Certainly I've always been interested in birds, at least for as long as I can remember. As a child I remember reading T. H. White's book *The Goshawk* and that's my earliest memory of my passion for raptors.

I most certainly can remember my first bird of prey, a Bonelli's Eagle smuggled into Gibraltar from Spain when I was in the R.A.F., while my second was a Goshawk I tried to train while living in Louveciennes, outside Paris when stationed at S.H.A.P.E.

My professional career began when I was Publicity Manager at Colwyn Bay Zoo, where I first suggested the flying of birds of prey in public displays, something which was then considered to be impossible according to Michael Woodford, the then Secretary of the British Falconers Club, an organisation that has consistently opposed any form of public display of falconry, except when done by their members at events such as the Game Fair.

Today, although I give regular displays to visitors to Leighton Hall, as I have done at both Weston Park and Chilham Castle, I prefer to work for children. Their enjoyment is obvious, their interest genuine, and their search for knowledge and interest in wild life most refreshing. I hope that, by flying some birds in front of groups of children I am able to give them some pleasure and above all arouse in them an interest in birds of prey and their conservation. If I can do that with just a handful then I'll be more than content.

Allan Oswald
Leighton Hall
August 1981

1   The author shows "Wally" his Wahlbergs eagle to the Mayor of Morecambe & Lancaster, Councillor John Lodge.

(Courtesy Lancaster Guardian)

CHAPTER ONE

The History of Falconry

To be thoroughly imbued with the liberal arts refines the manners,
and makes me to be mild and gentle in their conduct.

Ovid.

Falconry is the world's oldest sport.

It is uncertain where and when man first trained a bird of
prey, but it was probably in Scythia. Certainly, by 2,000 B.C.
the art was established in Persia, Arabia, India and China, in
other words throughout the civilised world of that time.

The Romans may have learnt falconry from the Greeks
but the lack of references in their literature would seem to
indicate that it was not very popular. It was certainly known
during the time of Vespasian, who at one time commanded
the Roman Army of occupation in Britain and who was
Emperor for the last nine years of his life (A.D. 9–79).
Martial (A.D. 40–104) referred to his hawks as fowler's
servants—indicating that falconry had gained some following. There are also some references to Caesar using
falcons to destroy pigeons carrying messages.

Ethelbert, King of Kent at the close of the sixth century,
who was best known for having accepted Christianity from
St. Augustine, wrote to Germany for a brace of falcons that
would fly at Cranes 'and bring them to the ground as there
are few such birds in Kent'. Later, Archbishop Mons
presented Ethelbert with a hawk and two falcons.

It is often wrongly claimed that Alfred (A.D. 871) was the
first English king to be a falconer. Possibly he was the first
king to train his own birds rather than rely on imported
birds that had already been trained. It has also been suggested that he wrote a book on falconry and although there

3

are numerous references to such a work in other writings of
the period, there is no proof that it ever existed.

Hunting in Saxon times tended to be a casual affair with
men hunting where game was plentiful. The Normans,
having completed the occupation, introduced a more
ordered society. Land ceased to be common property and
the right to hunt became the privilege of those who owned
land. The serfs had to rely on their masters goodwill or a
few public warrens for their meat. Although domestic
animals were kept in most villages and hamlets they were
valuable, and only killed for meat in exceptional circumstances, except in the autumn when all surplus animals were
slaughtered to save winter fodder. Using force when necessary, the Normans tried to impose their language and
customs on an unwilling Saxon nation but the need to
communicate was such that they were forced to make con-
cessions which led to the gradual development of a language
that was neither Saxon nor Norman, the forerunner of
modern English. That is why so many of our words have a
slightly French ring to them. 'Falcon' is derived from the
old French 'faucon' and 'hawk' from the Saxon 'haysc'.

In Norman times vast areas of the country were Royal
Forest, in fact almost a third of the country was forest, a
high percentage of which were of oak. It has been claimed
that there was so much forest that a squirrel could climb
into the tree-tops in Bristol and travel to the Wash without
once touching the ground.

Numerous laws were passed to protect the 'beasts of
the forest', Red and Fallow Deer and Wild Boar which
were known as the venison, while growing timber was the
vert. Only the King had the right to hunt venison in Royal
Forests but he quite often gave limited rights to hunt
greater or lesser game according to his fancy. Wolves were,
however, excluded from all protection and regarded as
pests to be exterminated. King John even went so far as to
appoint special officers to destroy them and in addition paid
a bounty of five shillings a head. When royal forests

encompassed an estate, the forests laws prevailed over the estate, unless the King gave the estate owner rights to hunt.

Villagers living in or near forests were allowed to graze their pigs and collect fallen wood—but not for two weeks before or after Midsummer Day, a time when the deer were fawning. In many areas 'venison' was protected by forest keepers who used 'club' law which forced the peasants to rely even more on their pigs and poultry as well as growing peas, beans and 'worts'. Bread depended on an uncertain harvest and was a luxury in most households which either replaced or supplemented it by grinding chestnuts to make a meal.

The fact that a man owned some land didn't necessarily give him the right to hunt rabbits, or coneys as they were called. To have the right to hunt rabbit, even on his own land, he had to be a Yeoman, a man who owned land worth at least £6 a year but who was not permitted to bear arms.

By 1389, poaching had reached such proportions that the Commons complained that artificers, labourers and servants often kept Greyhounds and other hunting dogs that were used to aid them when poaching. Consequently a law was then passed that prohibited any man with less than forty shillings a year in land, or a priest or clerk with less than ten pounds a year income to keep sporting dogs or nets.

Later, rabbits were regarded as a plague and could be snared and dug out from all but private warrens. For their hunting pleasures, gentlemen would hunt deer by horse and hound, fly their birds at pheasants, partridge and heron, or lie out at night to net fox and badger. At the same time, most hunting was carried out to provide edible meat rather than for the pleasure of the chase. Hawking was, therefore, more often than not an economic necessity more than just a sport.

In 1199, King John, to improve his personal hunting, forbade the taking of all feathered game in Royal forests; a law that if enforced effectively, would have caused a lot of hardship. To alleviate, outwardly at least, the suffering and hopefully smother the inevitable mutterings of the populace, he ordered that one hundred paupers should be fed from the proceeds of each hunt. This arrangement may have worked well for those living in areas that were frequently hunted, but it did little to help those living in the areas which the King never visited.

The Forest Charter, granted by Henry III in 1217, gave every freeman the right to have eyries of hawks, sparrowhawks, falcons and eagles in his forests. It made, however, no mention of any penalties for the theft of birds but, just over one hundred years later, Edward III made it an offence punishable by death to steal a hawk. This followed a proclamation, made three years earlier, that dealt with the procedure to be followed when a lost hawk was found.

How he shall use another man's hawk that taketh it up . . . Also it is ordained in this present Parliament that every person who findeth a falcon, tercelet, laner or laneret, goshawk or hawk that is lost by their Lord that presently he bring the same to the Sheriff of the County, and that the Sheriff make proclamation in all the good towns in the County that he hath such a hawk in his custody: and if the Lord who lost the same or any of his people from him come to challenge it, and proveth reasonably that the same is his Lord's let him pay for the costs and have the hawk. And if none come within four months to challenge it then the Sheriff shall have the hawk, making satisfaction to him that did take it if he be a simple man; and if he be a gentleman of estate to have a hawk then the Sheriff redeliver to him the said hawk taking of him reasonable costs for the time he had it in his custody. And if any man have taken such a hawk and the same conceal it from the Lord whose it was, or from his falconer, or whosoever taketh him from his Lord and thereof be attained, shall have imprisonment of two years and shall yield to the Lord the price of the hawk so concealed or carried away and if not the longer he shall abide in prison.

Edward III must have had more than a casual interest in falconry because when he invaded France his retinue included thirty mounted falconers. Even war, it seemed, was not to be allowed to interfere with Royal hunting pleasures. Later in 1361 Edward III made it a felony to take a hawk, or its eggs, even from one's own grounds, punishable by imprisonment for a year and a day in addition to a 'fine at the King's pleasure'. The term of imprisonment was later to be reduced to one of three months, providing the offender gave an assurance that the offence would not be repeated for seven years—an early form of probation!

Often quoted as belonging to this period is a punishment for hawk stealing:

Si quis acceptorum alienum involare proe sumpserit aut sex uncias carnis acceptor ipse super testones comedat aut certe si nolverit sex solidos illi acceptor est, cogatur ex solvere mulctae autem nomine solidos duos.

This probably comes from the legal code of the Burgundians in the sixth century since the word 'testones' appears in no other traceable source and all dictionaries of medieval Latin give only the single Burgundian source.

If someone should dare to steal another's hawk, either let the hawk eat six ounces of meat placed on the offender's testicles, or, if the offender prefers, let him pay six solidi to the hawk's owner, and a further two as a fine.

An alternative translation could read 'either let the hawk, placed on the offender's testicles, eat six ounces of meat.'

While, in England, falconry was a major pastime as well as being one of the main means whereby fresh meat was acquired for the family table, its development was following similar lines on the continent. In France the Grand Fauconnier was paid 4,000 florins for maintaining an establishment of some three hundred birds. In England the office of Master of Hawks was given to a man of high rank and was very well paid—in 1536 he was paid £40 and his under falconer £10 a year. Today the Grand Falconer of Great Britain is the Duke of St. Albans who used to receive £100 a year, that was until about fifty years ago when the House of Commons suddenly woke up to the fact that he was being paid for doing nothing! It would appear that the last time a Duke of St. Albans flew any birds in public was at Brighton in 1836.

Very little is known about the Office of the Grand Falconer of Scotland although some reference to the Under Falconer has been traced. The last man to hold this office, a Mr. Marshall Gardener, apparently retired in 1840. Other references that have been traced would appear to indicate that the major office was held by a man of exalted rank.

The Tournai Font, pictured below, is to be found on the north side of the nave of Winchester Cathedral. It may have previously stood at the west end of the Norman cathedral and was moved to its present location during alterations, and never, for some reason, returned to its orginal position.

It is made of black marble from the quarries on the River Scheldt near Tournai in Belgium.

For many years it was thought that there were seven such fonts in England but the fragment of an eighth was found near Ipswich. Today, similar fonts can be found in St. Michael's, Southampton, and the parish churches of East Meon and St. Mary Bourne.

All the fonts appear to have been carved in Belgium in about 1150 and brought to England by water. The one in Winchester could possibly have been brought over by Bishop Henry of Blois. The font is just over three feet high and about three feet square with the bowl large enough to completely immerse a child as was so often the case in the Middle Ages.

The figures carved on the side appear to include a bishop on the right and a falconer on the left. It should be noted that the falconer is carrying his bird on his right glove which would appear to have been quite common on the continent.

2   Detail from The Tournai Font—Winchestei
    Cathedral. Made of black marble from the
    quarries on the River Scheldt near Tournai in
    Belgium. It was probably carved in about 1150
    and transported to the Cathedral by water. The
    whole font is 3ft. high and 3ft. square and
    contains a bowl large enough to baptise an
    infant by total immersion.

Pennant, in his *Tours of Wales* refers to the laws of Hywell Dda (thar). Dda, which in Welsh means 'the good', lived in about A.D. 940 and who described, in some detail, the rights and privileges of the Chief Falconer to the Welsh Prince, which Pennant quotes:

Falconry was held in high esteem among the Welsh. Our Prince had his Chief Falconer, who occupied the fourth in rank among the officers of his court. The falconer was called Penhebogydd (Pen-neb-og-eeth) and was fourth out of the twenty-four officers of the Court taking precedence over the Judge of the Palace, the Head Groom and the Chief Huntsman. He held his lands free; had a double portion of provender for his horse; the Prince supplied him with woollen cloaths and the Princess with linen. He brought his cup with him into the Hall; but was not allowed to drink more than would quench his thirst lest he should get fuddled and neglect his hawks. He was allowed the hearts and lungs of all animals in the Royal kitchen, and sometimes a barren ewe to feed his birds. Whenever his hawks killed any of the three most noble species of game, the Heron, the Bittern or the Crane, he received from the Prince three services; that of holding his horse while he was taking the hawks from the game and of holding his stirrup again when he mounted his horse and at night the Prince honoured him with serving him thrice with his own hands.

In case the falconer took any of the Royal birds in the Prince's absence he was to bring it into the hall and shew it to him; on that the Prince was to rise, or if he did not, he was to bestow on him the robe he then wore. During the time that the hawks were in their mew (moulting) the falconer was not bound to answer any suit. If he killed his horse in the exercise of his office the Prince was to find him another. The fine for an injury to the falconer was vi cows and cxxvi pence. His slaughter was not to be atoned for less than one hundred and thirty-six pence.

Let me conclude with saying that there was a peculiar tax for the support of this office called Cylch Hebog-yddion (Killssh Heb-og-eeth-ion) which fell on the vassals; for the Prince contributed little or nothing towards the expence of his amusements.

The reference, as quoted by Pennant, to the falconer not being required to answer any suit while his birds were in mew could quite possibly have been wrongly translated. While a bird is in mew, the falconer has little to do since the bird requires no training or exercise. This would probably have been the one time in the year when the falconer could answer a suit since when taken from the 'mew' birds would require almost complete retraining making this a suitable time for a replacement falconer to take over.

There are numerous references to falconers being asked to 'mew' their birds in various barns. Barns are empty in the summer months and while moulting, the hawks would be freed in the barns and would probably thrive on the rat population, bearing in mind that in those days barns were totally enclosed buildings from which the doors were the only exit.

References to 'Bowshot' being used as a measure of distance are quite common but 'falcon flight' as a measure of distance is not.

There is an old legend dating from the Middle Ages that in about A.D. 980 the Danes landed in Perthshire and defeated the Scots who in their flight had to travel through a narrow pass. An old man and his two sons were ploughing nearby and arming themselves, the old man with the yoke that yoked his two oxen to the plough, they stationed themselves in the pass and slew all, Scot and Dane, who came past. This rallied the Scots, and led by the gallant three, they routed the Danes and saved Scotland.

The legend continues that the grateful king offered the old man as much land in the fertile Carse of Gowrie as a hound would run over or a falcon cover in her flight. He

3   The arms of the 'Hays' of Errol.

chose the falcon's flight, and the lands, extending to several miles, so covered became the lands of Erroll (in Perthshire) by the red Tay. The various ancient boundary stones of these lands are still held in local veneration and are called falcon's stones. At the westernmost stone (which can still be seen, and on which the falcon is said to have alighted on its return from the encircling flight) is a hamlet called Hawkstane. The easternmost stone is on what is now Lord Kinnaird's property at Rossie, where it is pointed out to visitors. Another stone was brought to Buchan when the Errolls sold Erroll in Charles I reign, and kept as a wishing-stone at Slains Castle. It is now at the Kilmarnock Arms Hotel, carefully preserved for the present Countess of Erroll by the kindness of the proprietors there.

When heraldry came in some time later, the three red escutcheons on the silver shield of Erroll were held to represent the father and his two sons, the three who shielded Scotland against the Danes. This explanation is probably fanciful (the arms first appear on the seal of David Hay, second Baron of Erroll, 1195–1230). But at the end of the Middle Ages the Errolls who had first used a stag's head for a crest, then a bull's or ox's head, assumed a falcon crest in memory of the old legend. At the same time they took an ox-yoke for a badge, and two savage countrymen wrestled and girdled in laurel (holding ox-yokes) for their supporters. Their motto has been, from time immemorial, SERVA JUGUM—PRESERVE THE YOKE.

An ancient prophecy about the Errolls, which has been attributed to Thomas the Rhymer, who lived at the close of the thirteenth century, is quoted by Professor Sir James Fraser in his work *The Golden Bough*. The Golden Bough is, he believes, a bough of mistletoe growing on an oak in the sacred grove.

> *Quhile the Mistletoe bats on Erroll's Aik,*
> *And that Aik stands fast*
> *The Hays sall flourish, and their guid gray Hawk*

Shall nacht flinch befoir the Blast.
Bot quhen the root of the Aik decays
And the Mistletoe dwines on its wither'd breast
The grass sall grow on Erroll's Hearthstane
And the Corbie roup in the Falcon's nest.

This prophecy was literally fulfilled when, after the fall of the Sacred Oak in the reign of Charles I, the lands of Erroll were sold out of the family. Gilbert Hay, eleventh Earl, was a minor at the time—and the lands were sold by order of his tutor, John Lyon, second Earl of Kinghorne and tenth Lord Glamis (the Queen's ancestor), who came of a family which has an all too familiar acquaintance with witchcraft and the pagan religion since his own ancestress Lady Glamis had been burnt as a witch less than a century before. He may well have hastened the oak's downfall and disposed of a property that could have linked his little nephew with odd doings from a forgotten past.

The prophecy was fulfilled when Lady Erroll visited the overgrown mound at Erroll, which formed the artificial base for the original wooden castle of her race nearly eight centuries ago, in the 1950's. As she approached, corbies flew out rouping hoarsely and there she found grass growing on what had once been Erroll's hearthstone.

(The foregoing was extracted from *Short history of the Hays or Erroll, in the Parish of Slains, in the district of Buchan,* published by the *Buchan Observer* in 1973. The history is based on notes compiled originally in 1951 by Lord Moncrieff. The information was kindly supplied by the Countess of Erroll.)

Birds of prey have been used for purposes other than as providers of food and instruments of sport. Sir John Stanley held a grant of the Isle of Man from Henry IV, to be held by his heirs and successors, by homage and the service of two falcons presented to the King on Coronation Day. Philip de Hasting held the Manor of Comberton in Cambridge by service of keeping the King's falcons.

Richard I is probably England's most colourful monarch. He took as many as three hundred birds with him on the Crusades and brought back equipment and ideas taken from the enemy. According to some chroniclers, such as Ambrose and Suba ad Din, Salhadin and Richard never met; in fact, when Richard's galley was approaching Acre and one of his birds escaped, it was taken 'prisoner' by Salhadin who refused to return it. This might seem trivial, but when viewed in the knowledge that knights taken prisoner would often refuse to barter their freedom in exchange for their hawks and falcons, it takes on a different light.

In the early twelfth century Ousama, son of the Lord of Shaizar, said that his father sent men into far off lands to buy falcons, and that his servants were mostly falconers or Saker Keepers and that his company of mamluks were all taught the art of falconry. He also describes how falcons were taken to springs to bathe after they had been hunting. The favourite bird was one that, though still young, was as large as an eagle. The head-keeper, Gana'im used to say that it was called Al Yashur and that it had no equal and eventually became like one of the household.

> If it wished to bathe it would move its beak in its dish to show what it desired and then my father would order a tub of water to be placed near it. When it came out, my father put it on a wooden gauntlet and set the gauntlet by a wooden brazier. The falcon was combed and oiled and then they rolled up a fur cloak for it on which it settled down and slept and it would be taken, as it slept, to my father's bedchamber, there to remain.
>
> Mamhoud, Lord of Hamah, would send for the falcon every year and it would be sent to him with a keeper and he would hunt with it for twenty days.

The works of both Father Rubruquis and Marco Polo give an indication of falconry's popularity among the thirteenth century Tartars. The Palace of Changa-nor, or the White Lake, was a favourite hunting resort of the Grand

Khan. 'The Grand Khan', said Marco, 'derives the highest degree of amusement from sporting there with Gyrfalcons and hawks.' At another palace near the city of Chandu, in Tartary, the Grand Khan kept upwards of two hundred hawks which, when he was there, he visited at least once a week. The mews were in a deer park where, to feed the birds, a variety of animals such as deer and goat were kept.

The Kublai Khan had two court officers of the highest dignity called Masters of the Chase. After residing in the metropolis of China he always proceeded to enjoy the field sports in the plains of Tartary attended by full ten thousand falconers who carried with them a vast number of Gyrfalcons, Peregrine Falcons, and Sakers as well as many vultures in order to hunt the game along the banks of rivers. The falconers used to operate in parties of two hundred or so, taking all kills to the Khan. Ten thousand guards were employed to keep watch, and a signal station or tent, raised on an eminence, received any stray birds that were caught. These annual expeditions were attended by the wives and ladies of the court who hunted with their own birds and retinue. The hunting was restricted to nobles with their own retinue with no one being allowed to hunt near the royal residence.

In Persia, according to Sir John Malcolm, the hunters went to a large plain or desert with hawks and greyhounds. The hounds were generally on a leash with their handlers also carrying a hawk. When Antelope were seen the hunters would try and get as close as possible, but when the animal broke the hunters would follow in full cry having first slipped the dogs. If they were hunting a herd, the hunters would wait until the hounds singled out an animal when the hawks would be released to fly at its head in quick succession, often with enough power to knock it over. The birds' aim was to slow the victim down to give the hounds time to catch up again. Although the hunting involved trying to catch some of the fastest quadrupeds, the runs rarely lasted more than three or four miles, so the dogs

4   One of the falconer's favourite falcons, especially in the Middle
East, the Saker.

could move in quickly and finish making the kill. Fawns
were never hunted being too easy and bucks were also left
alone as their horns could impale a bird so easily. The
hawks were known as Cherkh.

The Hubara are a species of bustard found on plains
devoid of cover, except for small shrubs called Geetuck.

Hunting parties of twenty persons flew two kinds of hawk, the Cherkh and the Bhyree which was cast when the quarry first took to the air. The hunting parties would ride in extended line with the Cherkhs being periodically un-hooded and held aloft to seek out game. The Speckled Hubars, head erect and wings outspread, would run towards the Cherkhs which would usually make several pounces at the head which were either evaded or driven off by the birds beak and wings. When the Hubara finally took to the air the Bhyree were cast. Flights were usually of more than a mile after which the hunted birds would alight to be killed by another Cherkh that attacked them on the ground.

The following is an extract from an article entitled 'Falconry in Soviet Russia' by Professor G. Dementrev of the Ornithological Museum of Moscow, which was published in 1958 in *Chasse au Vol*, the magazine of the French Falconers Club:

> Falconry was formerly well developed in Russia and in the Asiatic states between the sixteenth and seventeenth centuries. At the end of the eighteenth century it fell into disuse in the European states. Its fall was almost certainly due to the introduction and use of firearms.
>
> In spite of the devotion of falconers such as Constantin Haller who tried to form an association of falconers in which he was helped by such exalted personages as Prince Alexandre de Oldenburg, the practice of the art continued to decline. Only a few amateurs continued to keep the sport alive. (1880) In the hunting reviews however, there were still articles dealing with falconry to be found. Constantine Haller published a most in-teresting treatise on falconry and hawking in 1885. Its title in Russian was *Okhota s sokolami i jastrebami*. That work was all however, and it failed to revive falconry in European Russia.
>
> Fortunately this was not the case in Turkestan and the Caucasus where it was still being practised. In the

following pages I am going to give you an account of observations I made between 1941 and 1956 in Turkestan where I enthusiastically practice the art.

In Kazakhstan and the steppes of Kirghiz Golden Eagles and Goshawks are mostly used. Goshawks, the more popular with their distinct markings, winter in Siberia coming from the south. On the other hand Peregrines and Sakers and Gerfalcons from Altai and the north, are rarely used.

In Turkmenistan, like Iran, the Saker is the most popular bird. In the Amou Doria Valley Goshawks are used and less frequently the Golden Eagle.

In Turkestan falconry is not practised so much as a sport as for economic reasons, in this area wild fowlers specialise in the use of falcons.

Inhabitants of the Kirghizes and Kozakhstan steppes call the falconer 'Kutschi' and those who hunt with the Golden Eagle are called 'Berkutschi'. The inhabitants of Turkmenistan call a falconer's birds 'Jolkush', that is to say trained birds, while the Goshawk is called 'Kartschiga' with the Kirghiz calling it 'Kush' which means bird 'par excellence'. The white Goshawks which come from Siberia are called by the Kirghiz 'Tujgun' whilst true albinos are called 'Tundscheur'. To everyone the Saker is 'Itelgi', the Gyrfalcon 'Schumkar' or 'Sunkar' the native Peregrine is 'Latschin' and the northern variety of the bird 'Bahryn'. The Golden Eagle is 'Berkut' or 'Burkut' and the Sparrowhawk 'Kyrgy'.

Falconers birds are obtained in two ways, either from the nest or as adult birds when they are trapped in nets. The young birds are usually taken from the nest when their feathers are half grown.* Generally not all the young

---

* This appears to be a little earlier than is the case in the rest of Europe, when young are taken just before they are able to fly; long after their feathers are half-grown. In this country most falconers would claim that birds taken when the feathers are half-grown would become 'screamers', birds that, when adult, 'scream' for food every time the falconer approaches.

are taken from a nest, only one or two. If there is only one bird in the nest it is never taken. This control is necessary for the conservation of the species.

In Turkestan most falconers maintain that two working falcons are an asset rather than a liability. Eyass are more easily trained than the trapped birds which are, however, ultimately the better birds.

Among migratory birds birds that have had their first moult are most popular, but for hunting gazelle and wolves only the Eyass is used.

In Turkestan birds are trained the same way as in any other country. The Eyass is not trained until fully feathered. Adult birds are gradually introduced to men, dogs and horses. Goshawks are carried without hoods. Falcons and Golden Eagles always taking a great deal of training.

Hawks are kept in good health with meat from the 'Ak-Dschen', soaked in water or with 'Bortje', meat without fat. A trainer must be careful to judge the right amount of food. When in level flight the bird's breast bone should be protruding slightly.

With all falconers the essential part of a bird's training is accustoming the bird to the falconer's glove. It is here that the bird has all its meals which consist of 150–200 grams for the Goshawk and Saker, and 500–700 grams for the Golden Eagle, which hunts foxes and hares and with the best birds wolves. The Goshawk hunts duck, pheasant, partridge and hare. In Turkmenistan mostly water fowl and the occasional gazelle are hunted. Hunting is usually carried out on foot or from a horse. When hunting hare and gazelle 'Tazy' greyhounds are often used. All hunting is carried out after the moult, that is towards the end of November, and ends at the close of the normal hunting season.

In Turkestan and the surrounding country birds are carried on the right hand. Goshawks are always unhooded but falcons are not always hooded. To carry the Eagle the falconer has a wooden arm support the end of which rests against his leg or his saddle.

The Georgiens keep their Sparrowhawks during the Quail migration after which they are released. In Turkmenistan falconers don't release their birds until they have worked them for six or seven years. The Kirghizes keep their Eagles for twenty years or more.

Today, in Russia raptores are studied for scientific reasons and in the main for the protection of wild life. We hope that these studies will lead to a revival of 'hunting in the air'.

That article would seem to indicate that in the U.S.S.R. falconry suffered much the same fate as it did in the rest of Europe, that of a decline following the introduction of the sporting rifle. There, however, it was fortunately kept alive in some regions where it is still a viable proposition.

Frederick II (1194–1250) was a Holy Roman Emperor whose court in Sicily was a centre of culture and learning that attracted Jewish, Mohammedan and Christian scholars. Forced by illness to retire from the crusades in 1227 Frederick was excommunicated by Pope Gregory. However, he later sailed for Palestine and by skilful diplomacy gained possession of Jerusalem, Bethlehem and Nazareth. He was a philosopher and man of science who delighted in exploding superstitions. He founded the University of Naples, was a patron of the medical school of Salerno, and wrote a treatise on falconry that is still regarded as being one of the classic works on the subject. He gave Sicily a code of laws and was supposed to be the first man to advocate the development of a relationship between man and his animals as opposed to the very strict man and servant relationship that had previously prevailed. He brought a great deal of sophistication from the east to falconry in Sicily and Europe in general, which was, in time, to greatly improve Europe's hitherto rather crude and unfeeling methods.

The Royal Mews at Charing Cross were built by

Richard II in 1377, but were converted into stables by
Henry VIII in 1537. Today the Royal Mews house not
birds of prey but the Queen's coaches. In many of our older
cities we can still find streets and alleys that are called
'mews'. In London in particular many of these contain very
expensive but highly fashionable houses into which the old
mews have been converted. The fact that these buildings,
originally built to house birds of prey, still stand today
gives some idea of the value man placed on his birds.

Heron hawking used to be one of the favourite forms of
hunting for sport rather than for food. When the Herons'
movements had been studied the hunting party would fly
off a cast (pair) of falcons from the leeward side of the
Heronry and towards the Herons who, on seeing the birds,
would disgorge their food and ring up (climb in circles)
trying to keep above the falcons. Working as a pair the
falcons would try to bind onto the Heron's neck without
being speared by the rapier-like beak. Eventually when the
two falcons had managed to bind to their quarry their
combined weight would force it down to the ground so
that the falconers, who would have followed the flight on
horseback, could reclaim their birds and despatch or
release the Heron.

Tamed Herons were sometimes used as decoys having
first of all been force fed, and then their necks bound to stop
them from disgorging their food on the supposition that
the extra weight of a full crop would slow them down and
give the hunting falcons a better chance. At one time a tax
of thirteen shillings and eight pence was charged on all
imported Herons, an indication of the popularity of that
particular form of hawking.

Hunting the Kite used to be carried out on Alconbury
Hill not far from Huntingdon which is now a U.S.A.F.
airfield. In this case owls used to be used to lure down the
Kites. The owls would have had a fox's brush tied to their
legs to slow them down. Today all forms of 'luring'
possible prey into range of the falcon or any other bird of

prey is illegal. In fact the average falconer would consider the very thought of such action most unsporting.

Most books and magazine articles that deal, in any depth, with falconry's history refer to what we now call the laws of ownership. The impression usually given in such material is that the laws laid down what species of bird could be owned and flown by whom, which is rather misleading. These laws were really little more than a social custom evolved over a period of time and applied on social occasions rather than in the hunting field, when a man would work the bird most suited to the quarry, providing it was not a bird allocated to a higher rank.

A man planning a day's hunting would take hunting the species of bird most suited to the quarry he proposed to take with the exception that the custom demanded that he never carried a bird allocated to a rank higher than himself. The allocations had evolved more round the cash value of the birds themselves than anything else. Native birds found in our own woods and fields found low on the scale. The most useful of the native birds, the Goshawk, was allocated to the lowest order that was allowed to hunt rabbit, the Yeoman. While many works refer to the Gos as being cook's bird since it, more than any other bird, provided the meat for the family table. It was no error that made sure that all men with the right to hunt could own a Gos.

The 'laws' first appeared in writing in the *Boke of St. Albans* a treatise on Hunting, Hawking and Armour published in 1400 by the Abbess, Dame Juliana Berne. Her listing gave the Emperor an eagle or vulture (the vulture was probably the Lammergeier) the King, a Gyrfalcon, and the Prince, the falcon gentle. (Since the word 'gentle' was sometimes used to denote the male it is possible that the falcon gentle was the male Gyrfalcon.) The Duke had a Rock Falcon, and the Earl a Peregrine. (Peregrines nested over most of the British Isles but only those coming from the remote hard-to-reach areas were classed as Rock Falcons and famed for their size and courage. For many years

Peregrines taken from round Llandudno's Great Orme were Rock Falcons some even being sent to Lord Exeter at Burleigh.) The Squire had a Hobby; the Knight a Saker, and the esquire, a Lanner. The Lady had a Merlin (Mary Queen of Scots when imprisoned at Richborough Castle was allowed to hunt with her Merlins). The Baron had the Bastard and the Yeoman, the Goshawk. (The Goshawk had, indeed still has, a reputation for being the most awkward, cussed, temperamental and bloody-minded bird it can be the falconers lot to try and train, so if the Yeoman's bird, the male, has that reputation what other name could one give to the female of the species?) The Priest had a Sparrowhawk and his clerk the Musket or male Sparrowhawk, and to simply acknowledge the fact that he existed as a form of human life the knave was allowed the Kestrel.

The *Boke of St. Albans* appeared in about 1400 so we can assume that the 'laws' were well established by then. In 1239 buyers from the King were being sent to Norfolk to buy four Gyrfalcons and five Goshawks presumably at the 'fair'. Which would seem to indicate that in the early thirteenth century the laws were not established. The ports of Boston and Lynn were of considerable importance at that time as they were exporting wool to Scandinavia from where many birds came to be openly sold at fairs. Birds were also often used to make payments to the Crown. For example two Gyrfalcons would pay for a licence to export Lincolnshire corn to Norway. Details of this type of trading can be found in the *Calendar of Liberate Rolls* of the thirteenth century, and the trade in birds of prey is commemorated on the King John cup now in the Kings Lynn guildhall. This cup is one of the finest existing examples of the medieval goldsmith's art and portrays hawks and falcons perched on the fists of fashionable ladies or held by pages. It is generally assumed that the larger birds on the cup are Gyrfalcons.

Six Gyrfalcons and six gentle falcons (falcones gentiles)*

* Six gentle falcons. Modern translations would seem to indicate that the reference was to six male falcons since the use of the word 'gentle' when

were sent by King Haakon of Norway in return for the fine scarlet cloth sent to him from England. Henry III sent special messengers to Norfolk to collect the birds.

Haakon, writing about the birds, said that his falconers had spent two years in Iceland enduring unbelievable cold and hunger while collecting the birds, and that he hoped Henry would appreciate them as did his fathers and his predecessors, who were said to have valued them more than gold and silver.

Numerous tales exist which tell something of the value placed by man on his birds. When the Bishop of Ely left a church he was visiting in Bermondsey he found his favourite bird had been stolen from where he had tied it outside the church. He simply excommunicated the unknown thief.

It was not, however, until the reign of Henry VII that the law, for the first time, dealt with the theft of eggs. This was in 'an Act against the taking of Fesaunts and Partridges'.

> Also it is ordained that no manner of person, of what condition or degree he be, shall take or cause to be taken, be it on his own ground or any other man's the eggs of any falcon, goshawk, laner or swan out of the nest upon imprisonment for a year and a day and fine at the King's will, the one half thereof to the King and the other to the owner of the ground, and that the Justices of the Peace have authority by the present Act to hear and determine such matter as well as by inquisition as by information and proofs.

That Act also laid down a penalty of £10 for driving birds from their covers, the fine once again being divided.

---

applied to a falcon identified to the male or tiercel. However, this reference (falcones gentiles) could also mean the Goshawk whose modern scientific name is *Accipiter gentilis*. When the Goshawk was given its first 'scientific name' that name was falcones which was applied to all birds of prey. It was only later that 'accipiter' was introduced to indicate the hawks, etc., and Aquila the eagles, and so on.

Later Henry VIII made the takings of the King's nesting falcons, or their eggs a felony.

> It shall be a felony to take in the King's ground any egg or bird of any falcon, goshawk or laner out of the nest; or to find or take up any faulcon, jerfaulcon, jerkin, sacer or sacret, goshawk, laner or laneret of the King's and having on it the King's arms and vervelles and do not within 12 days bring or send the same to the master of the King's hawks or to have one of his falconers or to the chief of the shire.

The act also applied in much the same way to the theft of the King's deer.

It would appear that Henry's punishments were not a sufficiently strong deterrent because in 1563 Elizabeth I increased the penalty for poaching to three months imprisonment and treble damages to the aggrieved party and then, after imprisonment the offender had to 'find sufficient sureties for the space of seven years after or shall remain and continue in prison without bail or main prize until the surety was paid'.

Elizabeth also forbade hunting with hawk or spaniel in growing corn, other than one's own, from 1st April until harvest, upon pain of forfeiture every time, to the owner of the crops, forty shillings. Even this act seemed to fail because James I (1602–25) increased the penalty to one month in the common gaol and/or forty shillings fine for every pheasant or partridge. The number of witnesses required to secure a conviction was at the same time reduced from two to one.

To improve his personal hunting Henry VII (1485–1509) forbade all hunting in the Palace of Westminster, an area that now covers St. Giles Fields, Islington, Hampstead, Highgate and Hornsey Park. Offenders were to be imprisoned to 'be visited by such punishment as His Highness the King shall deem fitting'.

From the reign of Alfred (871–899) until that of

George III (1760–1820) hawking was one of the favourite hunting pleasures of all monarchs. James I (1602–25) was the only exception, preferring fishing with Cormorants and Ospreys to the more traditional sports. Mention of this Royal pastime is to be found in the diary of Hans Jacob Wurmser von Vendenheym who accompanied Lewis Frederick, Duke of Wartemberg, on a diplomatic mission in 1610. His diary, now in the British Museum, tells of a journey through Ware, Royston, Newmarket and Cambridge to Thetford where, on 7th May, they found the King 'amusing himself by hunting, fishing and fishing with cormorants'.

James maintained a regular establishment for his Cormorants on the river at Westminster and even went so far as to create the office of Master of the Royal Cormorants. This was first held by John Wood. Records in the Public Record Office give some indication of the size and costs of the establishment.

No. 3. 31st August 1618—James to Robert Wood. Advance of £66.13s. in part payment of the sum of £286 due in respect of the Cormorant houses, and making nine pounds etc. at Westminster, the ground called the Vine garden having been taken upon the lease of the Lord Danvers.

Other documents indicate that interest in the use of Cormorants for fishing spread to the continent making James something of a trendsetter.

14th October 1619—To Robert Wood whom His Majesty intendeth to send, with divers cormorants, to his good cousin, the Duke of Lorraine, the sum of £60 by way of imprest towards defraying the expenses in that journey.

20th August 1624—To Robert Wood, the sum of £98.8.6d in full satisfaction of the charges and loss sustained by Luke Wood, in his late travels, with three cormorants, to Venice, having been stayed in his passage thither, and his cormorants taken away from him by the Duke of Savoy.

Several factors were responsible for falconry's eventual loss of popularity and near extinction. The initial and possibly major factor was the introduction of the sporting rifle, a far more efficient means of killing animals for both the table and for sport. In their early days these weapons were both unreliable and inaccurate but had the attraction of being novel.

Other contributory factors were the fencing in of farm-land to improve agriculture generally. Although fences and walls were no deterrent to birds, they made it difficult for the falconer to follow the hunt and increased his chances of losing his bird.

A factor not often considered is the changing pattern of life during the Commonwealth when the Puritans held their sway and forbade many of the country's traditional pleasures. It is not apparently known if they stopped hawking for food, but some uses to which trained birds were traditionally put would almost certainly have been stopped. There was a slight revival of interest following the Restoration (1660) but the sport never regained its former following.

The popular belief gained from standard history books is that falconry was 'the' sport of the Middle Ages. This is misleading. Birds were often used to obtain food for the family, in fact they were possibly used for this purpose more than for simply enjoying the thrills of a hunt, so it was, very much, an economic necessity. Other forms of hunting, such as netting, would certainly have provided some meat but it is very doubtful if these, and the limited number of domestic animals kept on most estates, could have provided half the meat eaten at the table.

According to the *Libro del Infante* of Juan Manuel, a nephew of Alfonso X the learned of Castille, who reigned during the first half of the fifteenth century, the King's day, when he wasn't disturbed by urgent political matters, began with morning Mass and Office followed by military training. Dinner with his entire suite was followed by singing and reading the epics of National heroes. Then after siesta and vespers he would attend to affairs of state until nightfall. The Prince's routine was just as well regulated. After an early Mass the morning would be spent writing languages and history until dinner and then again between siesta and supper. Monday, Wednesday and Friday mornings were, however, spent hunting, hawking and on military exercises. On Sundays, the morning, after Mass, was spent on riding and sport, but not hunting.

Trained birds have frequently been used during periods of war. A wing of some 8,000 birds was supposedly used by Richard I in the Holy Land. A Master Falconer himself, the King is supposed to have introduced into this country the falcon's hood to which he had been introduced in the Holy Land. Later the owners colours were incorporated into the feathers on the top of the hood and were thus used to indicate ownership; an idea that was to lead to the use of colours on racing animals, etc.—a rather tenuous supposition.

In 1871 Peregrine Falcons were used to good effect when Bismarck (1815–98) besieged Paris. The hunters were, in this instance, being used in an attempt to stop messages carried by pigeon from reaching the exiled government in Tours.

Old family records have told us a great deal about family life throughout our history, and this has certainly been the case as far as falconry is concerned.

According to *Rex Ripuar*, 17th century values were:

An untamed hawk	3–0
A One year hawk	12–0
A Hawk that flies at cranes	6–0
A Goshawk	3–0

In various other Household Accounts we find the following entries.

Itm. the viij daye paied to Walshe for so moche money by him layed out for one goshhawke and ij fawcons — iij li

Itm. the iij daye paied in rewarde to Sir Richard Sandes s'vant for bringing of a Saker to the King at Hampton Courte — vs

Itm. the iij daye paied for ij dousin of hawks hoods at iijs iiijd le dousin — vjs viijd

Itm. the same daye paied to iij hawks gloves at vjs viijd le glove — xxs

Itm. the same daye paied for vj dousin gilte bells at iij corons le dousin — xliijs

Itm. the xx daye paied to Philip Clampe for the mete of ij hawks after the rate of ijd by the daye from the xx daye of Aprill unto the daye of Novembre — xxvs

Itm. the vij daye paied to John Evans for his bourde wages for one quarter due at Our Lady daye laste paste — xxxs vd

Itm. the same daye paied to one that toke up a Lanner that had been lacking a hole yere — xs

Itm. the laste daye paied unto Nicholas Clampe for keeping of a Lanneret called Cutte for one hole yere at jd a daye — vd

Itm. the xii daye paied to a s'vant of Maister Stevingtons in rewarde from bringing hawkes out of Irlande — xl s

Itm. the xxv daye paied to Walter in rewarde for a Jerfawcon the dyed — xl s

Itm. the xj daye of Marche paied to Garrat and Richard the fawconers in rewarde for finding the Herons — x s

The household book of Henry Percy, the fifth Earl of

Northumberland, commenced in 1512, gives some rather interesting prices of birds for the table. Not only the prices but the birds involved are of interest.

Capons at ijd a peece leyn (lean)	Perttryges at ijd a pece
Chickeyns at ½d a peece	Redeshankes j½d
Hennys at ijd a peece	Bytters (Bittern) xijd
Geysse iijd or iiijd at the moste	Fesauntes xijd
Pluvers jd or j½d at moste	Reys (Ruff) ijd a pece
Cranys xvjd a pece	Scholardes vjd a pece
Hearonsewys (Herons) xijd a pece	Kyrlewes xijd a pece
Mallardes ijd a pece	Pacokes xijd a pece
Woodcokes jd or j½d at moste	Wegions at j½d the pece
Wypes (Lapwings) jd a pece	Knottes jd a pece
Seegulles jd or j½d at moste	Dottrells jd a pece
Styntes after vi a jd	Bustardes (no price given)
Ternes after iiii a jd	Great byrdes after iiii ajd
Quaylles ijd a pece at moste	Larkys after xii for ijd

(the old style of writing amounts of money was to replace the last i in Roman numerals with a j. Up to 24 pence was usually written as pence, two shillings and more being written as shillings and pence. li indicated a libre or £1)

St. Bravo of Valkenswaard is the Patron Saint of falconers, Valkenswaard being the traditional home of many famous Dutch falconers whose reputation travelled the world over. A large tract of open country known as the 'Swaard' lay on the migration route of thousands of hawks and falcons and an industry developed round these routes. The migrating birds were trapped and traded the world over and with the supply of birds thus assured interest was awakened. Unfortunately much of the famous Swaard has now been developed and the last of the great traditional trapping families, the Mollens, have died out so ending a great tradition.

St. Bravo was a native of Hall, Belgium, and was accused of stealing a white falcon. Found guilty he was condemned to death but just as the sentence was about to be carried out, the falcon suddenly appeared to prove his innocence and he was freed.

Towards the end of the eighteenth century the sight of a trained falcon at work in the British Isles became something of a rarity. One of the few remaining active falconers being Colonel Thornton of Thornville Royal. An accomplished falconer, he managed to gather round him a number of adherents who had found it increasingly difficult to follow the sport in the grand manner in their native Yorkshire, due mainly to the growth of agriculture. The Colonel sold out and moved down to Wiltshire where farming progress was slower. There, in conjunction with Lord Orford he formed, in about 1775, a Hawking Club which thrived and by 1783 the club owned 32 Peregrine Falcons, 13 Goshawks and 7 Iceland Falcons. The fifty or so club members paid an annual subscription of between £30 and £40 and met in April to fly their birds at Kite and Rooks. The club died in 1838 although a number of its members still remained active falconers.

Operating from the Royal Dutch estate at Loo, with the King himself among the members, the Loo Hawking Club followed the defunct Hawking Club and attracted a number of its former members. The subscription to this exclusive club was one hundred florins and the season, spent hunting Heron, lasted from 15th May until about 10th July. The Herons that were taken were rung and released, if they were uninjured. In this way some birds were caught several times in their lifetime. Unfortunately even the Royal Patronage wasn't sufficient to stop the club from dying out in 1853.

With a membership that concentrated on Rook hawking, the Old Hawking Club was formed in about 1864. This club hunted the Wiltshire Downs in March and April, and then moved to Norfolk for a short season of Heron hawking with occasional flights at Grouse in Perthshire in August. This club died in 1878 and was replaced by the Falconry Club which died in 1926, possibly because one of its objects was to fly birds at bagged quarry as a form of public entertainment.

Formed between the two World Wars, under the patronage of Goering, the German Falconer's club, 'Deutscher Falkenorden' was formed in 1923. This club still thrives and is therefore the oldest club in existence today. It is generally accepted as being the premier organisation connected with the sport, a reputation gained, as much as anything, from the fact that when the club meets it hunts rather than simply talks birds. The British Falconer's Club was formed in 1946 and was, for a time, the only organisation that supported the sport in this country. The Welsh Hawking Club, an organisation for practising falconers is today very active in Wales and the North.

It would indeed be strange if a sport as old as falconry failed to leave its mark on our language. In fact there are in use today a number of words that were originally part of the falconers language and which have been adapted for use in our everyday conversation. Obviously the reverse has sometimes been the case and it is not always easy, or even possible, to tell in which particular context a word was first used.

Possibly the most interesting word that has almost certainly been adapted is now used in an abbreviated form. The falconer refers to an adult female bird as being a 'haggard' and the abbreviated form of that word requires no explanation. The falconer, when talking of his birds, refers to the male as being a 'tiercel'. In some of the older works, the spelling variations give us 'tercel' and 'tassel' while in some instances the male falcon is referred to as being a 'gentle'. When he is talking about a female, the falconer just ignores the question of sex. In other words a 'haggard Goshawk' is in fact an adult female Goshawk;

the male would be referred to as a 'haggard tiercel Goshawk'.

Shakespeare was undoubtedly a naturalist of some experience. Most of his works contain at least one reference to nature, even to hunting, and in the light of the knowledge of his age his references are technically correct. In his day falconry was still very much in vogue and his accurate employment of its terms proves that he had more than a mere passing knowledge of its practice. It is perhaps unfortunate that most students of the bard, be they willing or unwilling, fail to appreciate the full meaning and derivations of some of his passages. The one sport in which he had little or no interest was fishing.

Othello, mistrusting the constancy of Desdemona and comparing her to a hawk exclaims:

> If I do prove her haggard
> Though that her jesses were my dear heart-strings,
> I'd whistle her off, and let her down the wind,
> To prey at fortune. *Othello*, Act III, Sc. 3

In this instance he can only be using 'haggard' to refer to a normal healthy adult female, a female capable of having an affair, for which she would be 'cast out'. If she were witch-like as the abbreviated form of the word would now imply, then she would hardly be likely to attract the attentions of 'another man'.

A bird cast off down or with the wind seldom returns to the falconer because, especially in a light breeze, the bird has to travel a considerable distance in order to gain sufficient speed to enable it to return. When flying his birds the falconer will usually try to ensure that they both take off and land, as with real aircraft, into wind. Hence, 'let her down the wind' meant, in this particular context, to send her packing. In *Taming of the Shrew* (Act IV Sc. 2) Hortensio speaks of Bianca as 'this proud disdainful haggard' a reference that can just as easily use the word 'haggard' or 'hag' in a truly derogatory sense.

Most authors and poets place the eagle at the head of the diurnal birds of prey and its reputed post as King of the Birds has led to it being variously styled 'the Royal bird', 'the Princely eagle' and 'Jove's bird', while the power of its vision is such that we still use the phrase 'eagle eye' and more recently, under the influence of the western, 'hawk eye'.

An eminent French naturalist, Lacépède, calculated that the eagle's sight is nine times more extensive in range than that of the farthest sighted man. Modern science has proved him to be amazingly accurate through calculating the varying number of retinal cells. One of the oldest legends that refer to an eagle's sight deals with its power to stare at the sun. Pliny said that the eagle exposes its brood to the sun gazing test to see if they are all genuine offspring, while Chaucer, in his *Assemblie of Foules* says

> There mighten men the royal egal find,
> That with his sharp look persith the sonne.

and Spenser in his *Hymn of Heavenly Beauty*

> And like the native brood of eagle's kind
> On that bright sun of glory fix their eyes.

The eagle's power of flight is said to be no less powerful than its sight, large eagles being capable, it has been claimed, of carrying hares and lambs, not to mention young children. There is little doubt that the birds can carry animals equal to their own weight, possibly a little more.

> An eagle flight, bold, and forth on,
> Leaving no track behind.
>
> *Timon of Athens*, Act I, Sc. 1.

and Spenser in the fifth book of his 'Faerie Queene' says

> Like to an eagle in his Kingly pride
> Soring thro' his wide empire of the aire
> To weather his brode sailes.

The Romans regarded the eagle as a bird of good omen

and the Jewish historian, Josephus, claimed that the bird was chosen for the Roman standard because it was the most powerful of all birds.

> Coming from Sardis, on our former ensign,
> Two mighty eagles fell; and there they perch'd
> Gorging and feeding from our soldiers hands.
>
> *Julius Caesar*, Act V.

This incident is explained in a little more detail in North's *Plutarch*.

> When they raised their campe, there came two eagles that flying with marvellous force, lighted upon two of the foremost ensigns, and alwaies followed the souldiers, which gave them meate and fed them, untill they came neare to the citie of Phillipes; and there one day onely before the battell, they both flew away.

Not that the eagle, as an emblem, is peculiar to the Romans. Portrayed with extended wings it was borne by the Persian monarchs who themselves had possibly 'borrowed' it from the ancient Assyrians on whose banners it flew until Babylon was conquered by Cyrus in 538 B.C.

> I chose an eagle and did avoid a puttock.
>
> *Cymbeline*, Act I, Sc. 2.

In this instance the word 'puttock' is used to denote a bird of ill omen, such as the Kite or Common Buzzard, so presumably the eagle was referred to as being a bird of good omen.

In Izaak Walton's *Compleat Angler* a falconer discussing the merits of falconry with an angler says:

> In the air my troops of hawks soar upon high, and when they are lost in the sight of man, they attend upon and converse with the Gods, therefore I think my eagle is so justly styled Joves servant in ordinary.

The eagle was the Roman military ensign from the

second century before Christ. Usually it was small in size so that, as the historian Florus claims, it could be hidden to prevent capture. Apparently an ensign bearer, in the wars of Caesar, pulled it from the top of the gilt pole and hid it under his belt. The bird was not adopted as the Imperial symbol by the Roman Emperors until some time later.

In *Cymbeline*, Act V, Sc. 4, Sicilius, speaking of the apparition and descent of Jupiter on an eagle says:

> The holy eagle
> Stoop'd, as to foot us; his ascension is
> More sweet than our blest fields; his royal bird
> Prunes the immortal wing, and cloys his beak,
> As when his god is pleas'd.

The word 'prune' is obviously an early version of 'preen' or 'plume', a word that was used after 'prune' and before 'preen'. 'Cloys' is generally accepted as being a misprint for 'cleys' or in the modern form, claws or talons. Birds often raise a foot and whet their beaks against it, an action that used to be known as 'cloying' the beak.

In *Underwoods*, Ben Jonson says:

> To save her from the seize
> of vulture death, and those relentless cleys.

Used as a verb, 'to cloy' meant to satiate, or gorge as the modern falconer would say.

> Or cloy the hungry edge of appetite,
> By bare imagination of a feast?
>
> *Richard II*, Act I, Sc. 3.

In Spenser's *Faerie Queene* the word is written 'accloy':

> And with uncomely weeds the gentle wave accloyes'

and in his *Shepheard's Calendar*

> The mouldie mosse which thee accloyeth.

Although 'regal' the eagle was apparently not supposed to be without feelings as Tamora says:

The eagle suffers little birds to sing,
And is not careful what they mean thereby,
Knowing that with the shadow of his wing
He can at pleasure stint their melody.

Titus Andronicus, Act IV, Sc. 4.

As is only to be expected from a 'royal' bird the eagle was supposed to live a very long time and there is no shortage of legends to support this.

In the *Psalms*

His youth shall be renewed like the eagles

In point of fact, an eagle that lived in Vienna was supposed to have lived for 104 years, while one of the Dukes of Atholl is supposed to have had an eagle that lived to be at least a hundred years old.

An old French 'Riddle book' entitled *Demand Joyus* printed in English by Wynkyn de Worde in 1511, gives the age of the eagle as follows

What is the age of a field mouse?
A year. And the life of a hedge-hog is three times that of a mouse; and the life of a dog is three times that of a hedge-hog; and the life of a horse is three times that of a dog; and the life of a man is three times that of a horse; and the life of a goose is three times that of a man; and the life of a swan is three times that of a goose; and the life of a swallow is three times that of a swan; and the life of an eagle is three times that of a swallow; and the life of a serpent three times that of an eagle; and the life of a raven three times that of a serpent; and the life of a hart three times that of a raven; and an oak groweth 500 years and fadeth 500 years.

'Tirings' are those parts of food eaten by raptors that they are unable to digest—fur, feathers, bones, etc. which are later regurgitated in the form of a pellet. All birds of prey must regularly be given tirings, in other words dead animals on which to feed. If this is not done they will soon suffer from stomach disorders. It has been suggested by those who dislike watching birds feed off other animals that meat wrapped in cotton wool is an excellent substitute. Tirings also used to be small amounts of raw meat on bones given to birds to keep them occupied 'picking', while at the same time helping to keep their beaks trimmed to shape. Something that does not seem to be done today, although I am at a loss to explain why.

A bird that circles above the hunting-field is said to 'tower'. The word 'tower' has its modern meaning, almost certainly derived from the falconers usage.

> And, like an eagle o'er his aiery towers,
> To souse annoyance that comes near his nest.
>
> *King John*, Act V, Sc. 2.

'Souse' is possibly derived from the German 'sausen' meaning to rush with a whistling sound like wind, hence our modern word 'stoop' which has evolved into 'swoop' and which has an almost identical meaning.

Shakespeare was obviously a student if not a practitioner of falconry. When trying to assess his knowledge, however, it must be borne in mind that in his day everyone knew the basics of the sport. His use of the terms is always correct and would seem to indicate a fairly sound knowledge of both practice and theory.

In *Henry VI*, Part 2, Act II there is a scene at St. Albans with the King, Queen, Gloster, Cardinal and Suffolk out hawking.

'Flying at brook' obviously indicates the area being hunted. 'But what a point, my Lord, your falcon made', refers to the habit of many falcons of staying circling tightly above a point where quarry has taken cover. Such quarry would then be 'put up' into the air and 'served' for the falcon to kill. 'And what a pitch she flew above the rest', simply praises the falcon for flying higher than any other birds to a height from which she would 'tower' above the

rest, so we have 'My Lord protectors hawks do tower so well'.
Chaucer also refers to hawking when he says:

> Ryding on, hawking by the river,
> With grey Goshawke in hand.

To fully appreciate any reference to the falconer's voice
it should be remembered that he is frequently required to
attract his bird's attention, especially when it is in flight and
getting further away every second. He must, therefore,
have a carrying and powerful voice.

In a Latin volume published in Leipzig in 1788, a
Professor Schneider lists the qualities of a good falconer
as follows:

> *Sit mediocris staturae; sit perfecti ingenii; bonae memoriae;
> Levis auditu; acuti visus; homo magnae vocis; sit agilis et
> promptus/ sciat natare/ etc.*

He should be of middling height and even temper; he
should have a good memory, sharp hearing and eyesight
and a strong voice; he should be quick on his feet and
ready for anything; he should know how to swim (etc.)

Every falconer is supposed to have had his own special
call for his birds which is supposed to have sounded rather
like:

> Hillo, ho, ho, boy. Come, bird, come.
>
> *Hamlet*, Act I, Sc. 5.

Game preservation as we know it was unknown in
Shakespeare's time but laws to protect men's possessions,
including game, did exist. The pheasant is not, as many
people seem to think, a recent introduction, neither for that
matter is the rearing of pheasants for food and sport. The
pheasant was certainly to be found in this country before
the Norman invasion, in fact it has been suggested that it
was first introduced by the Romans. In a manuscript dated
about 1177 the following bill of fare was ordered by
Harold for the Canons' Households in 1059:

*Erant autem tales pitantiae unicuique canonico: a festo
Sancti Michaelis usque ad caput jejunii, aut xii merulae, aut ii
agauseae, aut ii perdices, aut unus phasianus, reliquis temporibus
aut ancae, aut gallinae.*

These were the allowances for each canon: from the
feast of St. Michael (21st September?) until Ash Wednesday (February) either twelve blackbirds or two magpies or
two partridge or one pheasant; at other times either
female geese or hens.

(The text gives no indication of the frequency of the
allowance.)

In his classic work on British birds, Yarrel gives an
extract from Dugdale's *Monasticon Anglicanum* according to
which the Abbot of Amesbury was given a licence from the
King to kill pheasants. This is dated about 1100. In his
account of a feast given at the enthronement of George
Nevell as Archbishop of York, Leland claims that among
other good things, two hundred 'fesauntes' were provided
for the guests. The Household book of Henry Percy,
fifth Earl of Northumberland, begun in 1512, contains a
reference to the birds:

Item: Fesauntes to be hade for my Lordes own Mees
at principall Feestes and to be at xijd a pece.

The Privy Purse Expenses of Henry VIII prove that
attempts were then being made to rear pheasants, although
there is no reference to how they were eventually taken, it
being generally assumed that they were taken in nets.

In Henry VIIth's time it was forbidden to take pheasants
or partridges with 'engines' in another man's ground
without licence in pain of a fine of ten pounds to be divided
between the owner of the ground and the prosecutors.

Speaking of Bianca, Gremio says:

Why will you mew her?
The Taming of the Shrew, Act I, Sc. 1.

and Tranio replies with:

> And therefore has he closely mew'd her up
> Because she will not be annoy'd with suitors.

The verb 'to mew' or 'to enmew' meaning to 'shut up' apparently owes its origin to the word 'mew' or 'mews', a place where birds of prey are kept. The base word probably originated from the Old French 'mue', to change or to moult. Originally the mews were the buildings in which birds were kept during the moult and today the building in which they are kept at night and in inclement weather. The falconer would stop flying his bird when it began to moult and would leave it loose in the mews until the moult was completed, a procedure still followed today by many falconers. By tradition the moult started at the beginning of Lent and ended at the beginning of August.

Today the word 'imp' conjures up the impression of a mischievous child and less frequently a witches familiar. In this context it is claimed that the word is derived from the Old English 'impa', a young shoot. To the falconer, however, 'to imp' is to repair a broken feather by a process known as 'imping'. The word, originating from the Old English 'impian'; the Old Norse 'impfon' and 'impiton'; the latin word 'impotus' or the Greek 'imphuein', means to graft or implant.

Imping is one of those operations carried out by the falconer that have not changed with the passing of time, although modern technology has improved the methods with the introduction of impact and other adhesives.

A pamphlet by Sir John Sebright entitled *Observations on Hawking*, now a collector's item of great value, describes the operation in some detail:

> When any of the flight or tail feathers of a hawk are accidentally broken, the speed of the bird is so injured that the falconer finds it necessary to repair them by an expedient called 'imping'.

This curious process consists in attaching to the part that remains an exact substitute for the piece lost. For this purpose the falconer is always provided with pinions (right and left) and with tail feathers of hawks, or with the feathers separated from the pinion carefully preserved and numbered, so as to prevent mistake in taking a true match for the injured feather. He then with a sharp knife gently parts the web of the feather to be repaired at its thickest part, and cuts the shaft obliquely forward, so as not to damage the web on the opposite edge. He next cuts the substitute feather as exactly as possible at the corresponding point and with the same degree of slope.

For the purpose of uniting them, he is provided with an iron needle with broad angular points at both ends, and after wetting the needle with salt and water, he thrusts it into the centre of the pith of each part, as truly straight and as nearly to the same length in each as may be.

When this operation has been skilfully performed, the junction is so neat, that an inexperienced eye would hardly discern the point of union, and as the iron rusts from having been wetted with brine, there is little or no danger of separation.

> If then we shall shake off our slavish yoke,
> Imp out our drooping country's broken wing.
>
> *Richard II*, Act. ii, Sc. i.

Another operation once performed by the falconer is now, happily, obsolete on account of the cruelty involved and the more than dubious value of the practice. In his *Book of Falconrie* of 1575, Turbeville describes 'how to seele a hawke':

> Take a needle threeded with untwisted thread, and (casting your hawke) take her by the beake, and put the needle through her eye-lidde, not right against the sight of the eye, but somewhat nearer to the beake, because

she may see backwards. And you must take good heede that you hurt not the webbe, which is under the eye-lidde, or on the inside thereof. Then put your needle also through that other eye-lidde drawing the endes of the thread together, but cut off the threedes endes neare to the knotte, and twist them together in such sorte, that the eye-liddes may be raysed upwards, that the Hawke may not see at all, and when the threade shall ware lose or be untyed then the Hawke may see somewhat backwards, which is the cause that the threed is put nearer to the beake. For a Sparrow-hawke should see somewhat backwards, and a falcon forwards.

Madam,

> I had rather seel my lips, than to my peril
> Speak that which is not.

Anthony and Cleopatra, Act III, Sc. 13.

Sir Emerson Tennant, in his *Sketches of the Natural History of Ceylon* when speaking of the Goshawk says: 'In the district of Anarajapoora, where it is trained for hawking, it is usual, in lieu of a hood, to darken its eyes by means of a silken thread passed through holes in its eyelids. This practice of seeling appears to be of some antiquity but has happily given way to a great extent to the more merciful use of the hood'.

The 'lure' is a device used to recall a falcon that has flown beyond the range of the falconer's voice or his whistle. Swung round by the falconer on the end of a line, it is 'attacked' by the falcon which, as a reward, eats the small piece of meat with which it is baited.

It used to be of various shapes and consisted merely of a piece of iron or wood, generally in the shape of a heart or a horseshoe, to which were attached the wings of some bird, usually a Jay or a Magpie, with the small piece of meat tied between them. By tradition the falcon is always trained to the lure while hawks and eagles are trained to the fist.

As falcon to the lure, away she flies.

Venus and Adonis.

The game at which falcons are flown is known as the quarry and by tradition various species of hunter are trained to various quarries. Gyrfalcons and Peregrines are flown at heron, duck, pigeon, rook and magpie; Goshawks to hare, rabbit and sometimes partridge while smaller birds, such as the Merlin and Hobby are flown at blackbirds, skylark and snipe. Today few of these birds are in fact hunted, the modern Falconer hunting only those birds not protected by law. The expression 'Cry Havoc' was a call to ignore traditional quarry and indulge in the slaughter of any possible quarry that moves:

> Do not cry havoc, where you should but hunt
> With modest warrant.
>
> *Coriolanus*, Act. iii, Sc. 1.

The cadge was used to carry a number of hooded birds at the same time and consisted of a simple framework of rectangular shape and very short legs. Crossed straps over the shoulders were used to carry it, the servant being so employed standing in the middle of the cadge which he steadied in his hands.

It would appear that the cadge was usually carried by a lesser servant, probably someone who could not be trusted with any other duties. Known as the 'cadger' he had to remain with the cadge throughout the day. Obviously the birds' owner was rarely present, so if anyone praised his birds the recipient was the cadger who probably swelled with pride, in fact, he probably gave the impression that he was responsible for the birds condition. His seeking praise to which he was not really entitled probably gave rise to the modern meaning of the word. In the interim the word 'cadger' was used to denote a common, lowly servant which in its turn gave rise to the use of the word 'cad' meaning a rather low type of person.

CHAPTER TWO

The Falconer's Birds

Proud Nimrod first the bloody chase began.

Pope.

There are, distributed throughout the world, about three hundred and fifty species of bird of prey, many of which have sub-species or regional variations. They can be found in the lowlands and highlands, marshes and deserts; only deep in the Arctic and Antarctic regions are they missing. Unfortunately however only a small percentage of these birds are accepted as being suitable for falconry, many have never been fairly tested either in their native lands or as birds imported into the British Isles. Throughout falconry's long history the falconer has always been able to find an abundant supply of popular birds. Only recently has the need for conservation limited his choice, obliging him to try those species he has previously ignored.

Before he makes a decision on the species of bird he is going to train the falconer must consider a number of factors that include the type of country over which he proposes to hunt and the intended quarry and his own experience. The ornithologist has divided birds, as man has divided all forms of life, into orders, families, species, sub-species, and so on, but the falconer prefers to keep things simple and sticks to the simple groupings he used long before Carl von Linne Linnaeus. The falconer divides all birds of prey into one of five groups or families, only three of which he regards as being suitable for falconry. Some birds which he finds hard to place are simply treated as 'half and half'—such as those birds he refers to as being hawk-eagles.

One group the falconer ignores are the scavengers; vultures and kites, birds that live off meat as do all raptors, but which are incapable of killing their own meat. I have, on occasion, tried to train birds from this group and without exception have found them stubborn if not untrainable.

Owls are also ignored, mainly because their natural hunting habits do not suit him. Contrary to the general belief owls do not restrict their hunting to the hours of darkness, rather they prefer dusk and dawn while some, the diurnal owls, hunt quite happily by day or night. There is no reason at all why owls could not be hunted early in the morning, a time that would give the falconer ample opportunity to recover a bird that was proving reluctant to being 'taken up' after a flight. In the Middle Ages, some species of eagle owl were trained and used for hunting rabbits, but the sport was by no means popular. I have trained and flown, in the afternoons, with some success, both the European and American Eagle Owls and on two occasions the much smaller Tawny Owl.

Of the remaining groups, falcons are the smallest in size. They are often referred to as *LONG WINGS* on account of the shape of their wings; long, narrow and tending to be slightly swallow-shaped. They are capable of high speeds and normally hunt other birds that are taken in the air at the end of a stoop or near vertical dive. Their beaks are usually quite short with a distinct notch or tooth on the upper mandible and dark round eyes behind which there is a moustachial stripe.

When hunting with a long wing the falconer takes the bird into open country where it is released and flies, in circles, to a considerable height where it continues to circle or 'wait on'.

With the advantage of height a falcon can see over a wide area and is therefore quite likely to kill some distance away from the falconer, especially when one considers that the hunt itself may cover quite a distance. No bird of prey is ever encouraged to 'carry' its kill so the falconer has to locate the bird with a kill, not expect the bird to bring it to him.

The falcon must therefore be hunted over open country where the falconer can see most of the ground level for several miles around, and at the same time it must be country that he can cross easily and quickly, either on horseback, or in this day and age more frequently in a Land Rover or similar vehicle. Suitable areas are few and far between, the most popular being grouse moors.

The Peregrine Falcon, *Falco peregrinus*, is, of course, the

5   The Prince of Falcons—the Peregrine Falcon (*Falco peregrinus*.)

prime bird in this day and age, only being outclassed by the totally protected Gyrfalcon, *Falco rusticolus*. The British Peregrine has always been regarded as the best of the world's Peregrines, or Duck Hawks as they are called in America, which now puts them under pressure from collectors on account of the very high price they can command on the black market. Nests in this country have been systematically raided for their young for a number of years, certainly since before 1954. Only recently has the matter received any real publicity, now simply because of the very high prices of about £1,000 per bird being offered.

Ignored by the media is the fact that as many nests are raided for their eggs as for their young. Only when the fine for taking the eggs or young birds exceeds their market value will the depredations decline. It is still not an offence to be in possession of an illegal bird, only to be in possession of a 'recently taken' bird.

'*SHORT WING*' is the name given by the falconer to birds in the second group. These are the Hawks or Accipiters. This group, as far as the falconer is concerned, contains birds from several scientific groups but mostly those, such as the Sparrowhawk, whose scientific name contains the title Accipiter.

As a general rule they have bright yellow eyes, fairly short beaks that lack the distinct notch or tooth in the upper mandible. They are more heavily built than the falcon and have short rounded wings. By nature they are birds of 'mixed country', roosting in woods and hunting in the open fields living off small mammals with but a few taking the odd bird.

The falconer classes them as being birds of the fist. Birds that are trained to answer to the fist alone and not, as is the case with the falcon, to both the fist and the lure. These birds are carried on the fist until a suitable quarry is spotted and then the bird is released, or cast.

Our most common native hawk is the Sparrowhawk, *Accipiter nisus*, a bird that is all too often confused with the

Kestrel. When hunting, the Kestrel is over an open space, and hovers, head obviously looking downwards and watching. The Sparrowhawk is, however, rarely seen except by the competent ornithologist who sees it flying swiftly along a hedgerow looking for small birds.

The most commonly trained member of the hawk family is the Goshawk (*Accipiter Gentilis*) a bird that at one time bred over the greater part of the British Isles and which was, for quite a long time, regarded as being extinct in the British Isles. In the last ten to fifteen years it has begun to make a comeback due mainly, it has been suggested, to the birds lost by falconers. All through the Middle Ages, there were probably more trained Goshawks in this country than any other bird. Most mews would have held more Goshawks than falcons, for what other reason should the bird have gained the title of 'Cook's Bird'?

For hunting however, I prefer to work with the American Redtailed Hawk, *Buteo jamacensis*. The Gos, when on the fist, will often bate and fly at a leaf being moved in a light breeze. The Redtail, on the other hand, will pause for that odd second or two and make sure that the flight is worth making before taking off from the glove. Being a far steadier bird on the fist it is also much easier to train and control than the Goshawk.

Buzzards are not normally regarded as being suitable for falconry since few are real hunters. They are often confused, in the air, with the similarly shaped but longer-necked eagles. The Common Buzzard, *Buteo buteo*, is quite often trained by the novice and on rare occasions will take a rabbit. The American Redtail, *Buteo jamacensis* is really a buzzard, but in shape and habit is much better classified as a hawk.

True eagles are not half as popular with the falconer as most people would like to think. Their weight and size obviously goes against them and they have the added disadvantage of being rather difficult to train. In poetry and literature they are treated as being the King of Birds. Large and powerful-looking they may well be, but they are really scavengers who would much prefer to eat dead animals than hunt and kill for themselves. Much maligned birds, most, like our own Golden Eagle, are accused of a wide variety of crimes including killing lambs and carrying off young children. It is not disputed that they will feed off dead lambs and may kill the occasional very weak lamb, but a sound, healthy lamb is quite safe.

Golden and Imperial Eagles, *Aquila chrysaetos* and *Aquila heliaca* are probably the most commonly trained eagles with the Tawny or Steppe eagles coming a close second. Both the Tawny and Spotted eagles can make quite

6   Golden Eagle.

useful hunters. As a general rule it can be argued that on account of their weight and power eagles are neglected.

Stringent rules and traditions used to dictate when a bird was 'taken up' for falconry. Today these conditions are regarded as outlining the ideal rather than only conditions— a change that has occurred through force of circumstance rather than by the will of the falconers.

The youngest bird to be taken for falconry is the 'eyass', a bird taken straight from the nest. The eyass is removed as soon as the feathers are fully developed and just before the eyass leaves the nest of its own accord. Some of the old falconers used to claim that they could judge just when a bird was going to fly and so remove one from the nest the night before. A bird that is taken too soon becomes a 'screamer', a bird that never loses the 'baby' habit of screaming and begging for food, baby fashion, every time it sees the falconer. To the casual observer, this might seem to be an appealing habit, but to the falconer it is rather nerve-racking to say the very least.

The word 'eyass' is probably derived from the name given to the raptors nest, the 'eyrie' or, it has been suggested, from the old French, 'nias', a nest.

> There is, Sir, an aiery of children, little eyases,
> that cry out.

Hamlet, Act ii, Sc. 2.

When taken from the nest, the eyass is placed in the mews on a mock nest and left with an ample supply of food to settle in with its new surroundings. The nest is usually at one end of the room and some branches, suitable for use as perches, are located at the other end. All projections such as nails and pegs are removed and the windows covered with thin slats placed about two inches apart which must be vertical rather than horizontal, because a bird can perch or at least try to perch on horizontal slats.

Once a day, all old food is removed and fresh food left in its place. The bird is left alone as much as possible, and then, once it has settled in, the falconer visits it for short and then longer periods so that it gets used to him.

A bird slightly older than the eyass is known as the 'brancher' or in older terms a 'rammage'. These are birds that have left the nest and which are still learning to fly.

A 'Lenten hawk' 'Lantiner' or 'Lentiner' is a bird taken or trapped during their first 'Lent', in other words when they are approximately twelve months old. They are words that are seldom used today when birds taken at any stage of their juvenile plumage are known as "Passagers'.

The area in which the falconer lives is most important. No one living in a built-up area should keep a bird of prey. During the daytime, birds must be kept out of doors in a garden, most certainly not in the backyard. They must be trained in open fields. and not in the local park where they will attract attention from passersby and, almost certainly, be the subject of complaints to the R.S.P.C.A. and local authorities. The falconer should also be someone who has a fair amount of free time during daylight hours, in other words, someone who works irregular hours—such as a policeman. Those who work nine to five cannot look after their birds properly, being unable to give them daily exercise during the winter months.

As hunting birds, the eyass and branchers are reputed to never gain their full hunting potential. In the wild such birds are taught how to hunt by their parents. If they are taken from the nest then they never have the benefit of this tuition and only learn through trial and error guided by instinct, and that takes time once the bird has been trained.

The adult bird is the 'haggard'. By far the hardest bird to train, but also, without a doubt, the most efficient hunter. The haggard has hunted for its own food for some time and would almost certainly never have lived to reach maturity if it was not an efficient hunter. In practical terms we usually find that the 'eyass' and 'brancher' are trained by the novice.

It should always be borne in mind that a bird of prey cannot be trained to kill any animal that, in the wild, would not form part of its natural diet. It has been more or less proved that a bird's diet is determined by the food given to the bird as an eyass on the nest. Furthermore, it would appear that a species' diet tends to vary from region to region, being governed by the type of food most readily available during the nesting season. If, for any reason, a bird changes its territory, there is no guarantee that it will survive. It usually moves to an area with the same type of food that it was fed as an eyass. Healthy adults moved to a new region have been known to nearly starve before changing their diet.

Kestrels usually feed on small mice and voles, but the Kestrel family living high on the windswept Fells may well find mice and voles rather rare, and live, instead, off small birds. This is a situation that almost certainly exists in many of our city parks where 'Kes' has taken up residence. Mice and voles are scarce but there is a never ending supply of sparrows and other small birds.

A fact that does not appear to be considered by the many well intentioned ornithologists who rear foundling owls and the like, is that before releasing such birds, they must try and ensure that they are being released into an area where they can feed off the same food as their parents gave them on the nest.

The falconer has long appreciated that the eyass can sometimes be 'encouraged' to hunt animals that it would normally only take when nearly starving. In other words, the food given to the bird before and during hacking has some bearing on its future value as a hunter.

That is why, particularly in the Middle Ages, a hawk destined for hunting rabbits for the pot was fed on rabbit, and the female, destined for the tougher hare, was fed on hare and not encouraged to hunt rabbit.

Taking this a stage further, the old falconers used to 'blood' their birds by flying them at bagged quarry. Rabbits would be snared and then released in a situation where the novice hawk could hardly ever fail to make a kill. More

7 Kestrel (*Falco tinnunculus*). One of the most intelligent and amusing members of the falcon family and which, although usually spoken of as the 'beginners' falcon, is a bird that needs a great deal of time and patience to train properly.

often than not, that first flight was made at a rabbit that, in some way, had been slowed down. Today, of course, such goings on are illegal.

All too often the dainty little Kestrel is referred to as a hawk when it is a member of the falcon family. This error stems back, in part, to the fact that many of its local names use the word 'hawk'. Members of the falcon family have a notch in the upper mandible, present in the Kestrel, hawks and eagles do not. Early classification of birds and animals tended to refer to all birds of prey as being hawks; all, that is, except the eagles and vultures.

When science corrected this 'error' the dictionaries did not, thus increasing the confusion. No matter what the dictionary might say, it is about time the B.B.C. Natural History Unit, and the media in general, used words in their correct modern context, not as it was a hundred years ago.

The most common local name for the Kestrel is 'Hover-hawk' on account of its habit of hovering over hunting areas. In Sussex, however, it is the 'Fan-hawk'; in Yorkshire, the 'Mouse falcon'; in Somerset, the 'Vuzzy kite' and in Shropshire it is the 'Kastril' and 'Ketchie', words which are probably derived from the now obsolete names Castrel and Coystril. In Cheshire it is still sometimes known as the Stangall, which is probably a spelling variation of another obsolete name 'Steingall' or 'Stannel-hawk'.

Many falconers claim that the Kestrel is the ideal bird for the novice falconer. It is certainly the easiest of all birds of prey to train, but once trained it is of no value since no falconer is going to be satisfied with a bird that hunts mice!

> And with what wing the stanniel checks at it!
>
> *Twelfth Night.* Act ii, Sc. 5.

The use of the word 'check' in this instance almost certainly refers to the bird's habit of hovering over quarry.

CHAPTER THREE

The Falconer's Furniture

Despite its long and colourful history, the theory of falconry and the equipment has changed very little. Most of the changes in training methods have been made for humane reasons and changes in the furniture are usually due to the use of the more modern materials.

Before any bird is acquired, suitable accommodation must be available, and for the bird itself, the various trappings that make up its furniture must be ready, or at least the necessary materials be to hand ready for their manufacture.

This small booklet is only intended to provide general information; it is not a textbook from which the novice can train a bird, and it must not be used for that purpose. To prevent it from being used as a textbook, certain essential details have been deliberately omitted.

The first consideration when acquiring any animal must be its accommodation. For the bird of prey two 'homes' have to be prepared, one for use during the daytime and a second for use at night and in inclement weather.

The *MEWS* are buildings whose size depends on the number of birds to be housed at any one time. As a very rough guide, a minimum floor space of forty square feet is required for each hawk or eagle, and about half that for a falcon. Although the falconer may intend to own only one or perhaps two birds, he should be prepared to house more as he will probably find other injured or waif birds being brought in for attention. The floor area of forty feet per bird does allow for a population increase on a temporary

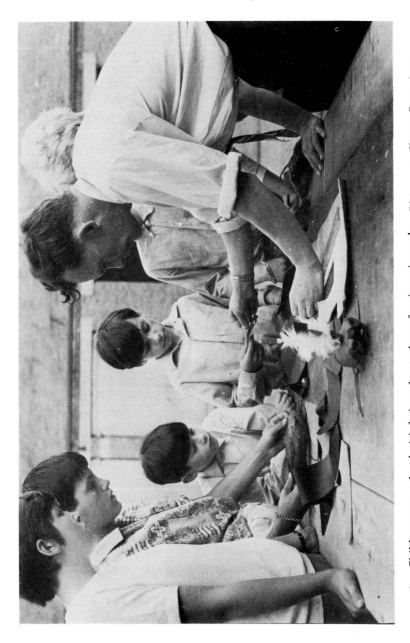

8 Children on a school visit being shown how furniture is made. *Photo courtesy Keystone Press Agency*

basis, no more, but the minimum floor area for a single bird must be at least ten by six feet.

The mews floor should be of well rendered and water-proofed concrete and must be sloped to a drain for rapid drying after the daily scrubbing out. The drain outlet should be provided with a 'plug' to prevent draughts in winter while the addition of closable floor level vents will also help in drying the floor.

The bottom three feet of the walls are also rendered smooth so they can be scrubbed and disinfected. The mews should have large windows with small panes and be covered with netting screens when open. It is just as important to keep local cats out of the mews as it is to keep any escaped birds in. If a bird is to be given freedom of the mews then the windows should be protected with wooden slats about an inch apart and running vertically. These will stop any loose birds from battering their heads against the glass in any efforts to escape.

It is a regrettable necessity that burglar alarms are now essential on all mews doors and windows. These can, with a little ingenuity, easily be made to operate either from the mains or batteries, using micro switches for the doors and windows and a transformer operating a relay to switch the alarm on. Once it rings, the alarm cannot be shut off by closing the mews door or window, only by closing the relay by hand.

The need for an alarm arises from the introduction of licences covering the importation of birds which has forced up the price of birds available for sale in this country by over 500 per cent. Anyone known to have birds of prey is at risk and very few stolen birds are ever recovered. This is a situation that will only be altered by the issue of licences to both obtain and keep birds of prey.

During the summer months, birds are only kept in the mews at night, during the day they are outside on the weathering ground.

THE *WEATHERING GROUND* is where birds are

perched during the day. It is usually located in a sheltered part of the garden within sight of the house so the bird can be checked at regular intervals. Whenever possible, I have available an ark-like shelter from the sun, wind and, of course, rain, which has a perch running from front to back. Most falcons like to bathe, so facilities must be made available which must be large enough to give the bird room to bathe without risk to its wing feathers. I move the perches about once a week so that the birds do not live on the same piece of ground. By moving them round the bath, the risk of infestation by worms and other parasites is lessened.

BLOCK PERCHES are the simplest form of perch used by the falconer and are the most widely used. In its simplest form, it's no more than a log with a metal rod driven into its centre. They should, however, be constructed with the aid of a lathe with which they are tapered

9a Ring perch.　　　　　　　　　　　**9b** Block.

inwards towards the bottom, thus making sure that the sides are never fouled and the tail kept well clear and protected. I have found that the best timber is teak which can be kept well oiled with linseed for weather protection.

Cork tops are easy on the feet and tend to lessen the risk of a foot infection known as 'bumble foot', but should the talons get a little too long then a block with a concrete top may be used to wear them down a little.

Other perches used on the weathering ground are the *RING* and the *BOW PERCH*. The ring perch is a modern adaptation, in metal, of the much older bow perch which probably gets its name from the fact that men would often stick their bows into the ground and use them as a perch.

The ring perch is best made with the aid of the local blacksmith and consists of a metal ring with a stem and 'trident' for sticking into the ground. A metal ring is fitted

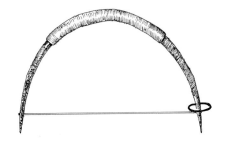

10a Bow Perch.

10b Screen Perch.

round the stem and to this the bird is tied. The top of the perch is padded with either strips of wood screwed into place or by bindings of leather.

As the name implies, the bow perch is a bow of wood stuck into the ground on which the bird perches. Once again the top is padded. To help the bow keep its shape, a 'stringer' is fitted between the two ends, leaving enough of the perch to be stuck into the ground. A ring, large enough to pass easily over the whole perch, is fitted before the stringer and it is to this that the bird is tied.

It has been suggested that, in the Middle Ages, branches were bent into shape while still growing and then, when they had reached the desired thickness, were cut and dried before getting a final shaping. Elm, because of its resistance to rotting, could well have been used.

In this day and age, the falconer is hardly likely to think far enough ahead to bend his saplings for later use as perches and so has to make them from scratch. Suitable timber can be 'steamed' and bent, an art that requires some practice. My bow perches are laminated from strips of marine plywood glued with a waterproof glue such as Cascamite. They are made round a metal former. Once the glue has cured, they are sanded and then varnished, being revarnished every spring. One perch made in this way was in constant use out-of-doors for three years and still showed no sign of weakening between the strips.

Every perch has to be designed with the bird's safety in mind. No matter what the bird does, it must be impossible for it to get tangled up round its perch, which is why birds are always tied to a ring which swivels freely round its stem. On the ring perch, the bird must be prevented from jumping through the ring, so this is 'closed' by crossed leather straps. The bird can, however, walk through the bow perch which is designed so that the ring can pass freely over the whole perch.

The perch used most extensively in the mews is the *SCREEN PERCH* which is really little more than a screen whose top is about waist high. It must, of course, have a firm base, even to the extent of being fixed to the floor. The width of the top depends on the birds it is to serve, being wide enough to give them a firm grip without their talons being completely wrapped round the whole perch. Some falconers will advocate a recess in the top, designed to accommodate the 'ball' of the foot to lessen the risk of bumble foot and other troubles. It is best if the top is made from a close-grained hardwood such as oak. With or without the centre groove the edges must be well rounded and sanded smooth. It is a good idea to vary the width of the top along its whole length, thus, if a bird is tied at one point one day it can be moved to its 'opposite' the next day thus varying the bird's grip.

Essential for the bird's safety is the screen of hessian or any fairly tough material stretched as tight as possible over the centre. This serves two purposes. Firstly, it is to prevent the bird getting tangled up around the perch when it jumps off one side and then climbs up the other. Secondly, the material will give the talons something easy to grip so that when it bates off its perch it can easily climb up again.

Birds are usually secured to the screen with the swivel held firmly on top of the perch. The normal procedure is to divide the leash into two in the centre and tie off at the swivel. The bird is then tied to the perch using a knot that can easily be undone but which is devoid of any loops in which the bird can get caught. Traditionally a type of falconers knot is used and the surplus leash wrapped round and round the only loop, thus sealing it off so that no matter what the bird does it cannot possibly get tangled up.

Screens are usually placed about three feet from the wall so that any droppings fall on the floor and not down the wall. When positioning their perch, many falconers forget that an eyass has a 'range' of about three feet or more, and whilst mutes can be easily scrubbed off the floor, it is much harder to try and clean them from off a wall.

Throughout the summer months perches and screens are washed and disinfected at least twice a week.

THE BIRD'S EQUIPMENT. The equipment used on the bird, known to the falconer as the bird's furniture, is normally made of leather. Every item must be inspected regularly since, if it is allowed to dry out, it will soon crack and then break, resulting in a lost bird. Although advertised for sale in a number of magazines, it is easily made and should always be tailor-made for each bird. Most escapes these days are due to faulty furniture, a sure sign of neglect on the part of the falconer. Items that are made of leather should be made of buck skin, a leather that appears in this day and age to be almost unobtainable. In the Middle Ages it was by far the most popular, being replaced in some cases with dog skin, equally unobtainable in this day and age! Most saddlers have a box of leather off-cuts and this will usually produce some suitable pieces. Leather must always be soft and supple and, most important, weather resistant.

THE JESSES are leather straps, one of which is attached to each leg. Once in place, they are never removed except to be replaced. They are joined at their free end to a swivel so they must be long enough to give the bird complete freedom of leg movement. When the bird is placed on the fist it is held by the jesses so they must also be long enough to be held in the fist when the bird is perched on it.

Jesses that are too short restrict the bird's leg movements and prevent it from scratching; but if they are too long there is a risk that they will slip on either side of the bird's block and so trap it.

Most books show jesses as having the part that goes round the bird's leg twice the width of the rest, and with the top and bottom cut into a series of serrations so that the leather tends to curl outwards, preventing the edges from hardening and cutting the bird's leg. The jesses should, again according to most books, be greased daily. To my mind this can lead to more problems than not greasing them. Leather, with age, tends to crack. If the jesses are greased daily their life is certainly increased, but I maintain that due to the grease the cracks are far harder to spot and may easily be missed resulting in a lost bird. I usually grease jesses when first fitted and only about once afterwards, but then my jesses are replaced at regular intervals, about once in every two months.

Turbervile, in his *Book of Falconrie* published in 1575, says: 'Shee must haue jesses of leather, the which must haue knottes at the ende, and they should be halfe a foote long, o there about; at the least a shaftmeete betweene the hoose of the jesse, and the knotte at the ende, whereby you tye the hauke'.

Modern jesses are not tied but then in the sixteenth century swivels, as used today, were unknown.

The distance between slits *b* and *c* is equal to the circumference of the bird's leg with a little bit added to provide the 'slack'. The slits themselves are as long as the jesse is wide. These can most easily be made by marking

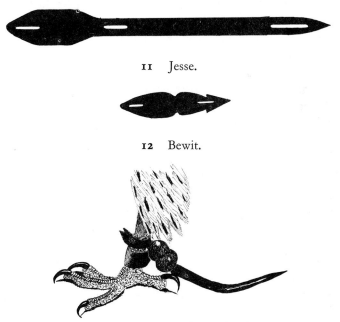

11 Jesse.

12 Bewit.

13 Leg with jesse and bells fitted.

the ends with a small punch and then joining the two holes with a sharp knife or razor. The length of slit *d* is equal to the diameter of the largest ring on the swivel.

Rather than risk wasting leather on jesses that are either too slack or too tight, 'test' jesses can easily be made from brown paper toughened with sellotape on one or both sides.

To be jess'd a bird should be carefully wrapped in a towel and laid on its back on a cushion. Care should be taken to ensure that there is only a single layer over the bird's head. One leg is freed at a time and jessed. A bird can quite often be calmed if a pencil or other suitable object is given to it to grip in its talons.

The section between *b* and *c* is placed round the leg and point *a* passed through slit *c* as far as slit *b*. With these two slits lined up together, end *e* is passed through them both and the whole of the jesses pulled through.

When first fitted, jesses should be fairly tight round the bird's leg, but not so tight that they will not slide up and down. It will be found that, with use, they will stretch and loosen.

With both legs jessed, the swivel is fitted. For small birds, such as the Kestrel, deep-sea fishing shops often provide nice light swivels, but failing that most good pet shops sell swivels and clips for cat leads which are ideal when the clip has been removed. Larger birds obviously require larger swivels. The centre pin is the weak point with all swivels and since cheap metal is usually employed, the holes are liable to wear. These swivels, which only cost a few pence, should be changed at least as often as the jesses.

Fitted directly above the jesses, by much smaller leather straps known as *BEWITS* are a pair of small brass *BELLS*. These are pitched with a semi-tone difference between them so that they produce a slightly discordant note that carries further than a single note. The function of the bells is to enable the falconer to locate a bird that has landed in long grass or other cover where it cannot be easily seen.

Most bells are imported from Lahore and are hand made

by local craftsmen from local brass that is workable, but at the same time durable with a remarkable tone, due mainly to impurities. European bells have never been made to a comparable quality.

Modern technology has produced small transmitters that enable birds to be tracked with receivers, but these are very expensive and although efficient lack the traditional character of bells.

To an experienced falconer the sound of his bird's bells are a means of communication. Although inside his house and out of sight of his bird he can tell, by the sound of the bells, exactly what his bird is doing.

The bewits are simply made of leather similar to that used for the jesses.

The jesses are fitted to the *SWIVEL* by passing end *e* through the swivel's ring as far as slit *d*. The whole of the swivel is then passed through the slit which secures the jesse in place. The same procedure is then followed with the other jesse, both jesses being passed through the same ring. Some falconers find it easier to pass both jesses over the swivel at the same time, in which case the jesses are passed through the ring and then end *e* of one jesse is passed through slit *d* in the other, and the two slits linked so that the swivel will pass through them both at the same time.

THE LEASH is the final item of furniture used to secure the bird. Made of leather with a knot at one end it is passed through the free end of the swivel and then tied to the perch, and is usually about a yard long. This length gives the bird a reasonable amount of freedom of movement round its block, but not so much that when it gains speed flying off its perch there is a risk of it injuring its legs when suddenly brought to a halt. Some falconers lessen the risk of injury by gathering a short length of leash and inserting a length of elastic. Should this break there is no risk of the bird escaping since the leash is left intact.

Recently, however, leather has been replaced by nylon webbing which is much stronger and lasts a lot longer. In nylon, the knot is made by rolling a length of the leash into an ovoid shape and then drilling two holes through the knot. The distance between them is equal to the width of the leash. The button is then unrolled and the holes joined with a sharp knife and the edges welded with a heated knife end or screwdriver. A leather leash is made the same way, only

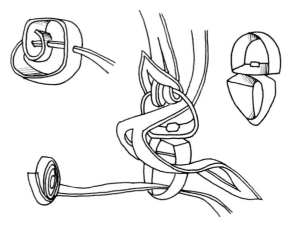

14   The swivel showing how the jesses are fitted and the leash made.

the end section of the leather is usually double the width of the leash so the leash itself does not have to be twisted through ninety degrees to pass through the button as is the case with the nylon webbing leash.

THE FALCONER'S KNOT can be tied with one hand. A bird should always be held on the fist while the knot is tied and when being taken up is again held on the fist while the knot is untied.

The knot is tied as follows:

1. With the bird held on the left hand, the end of the leash is passed through the ring on the block or perch, from the top, for about a foot.

2. The loose end is taken between the end of the first and second fingers and the leash held taut.

15a   15b

3. The thumb is placed over the leash running to the bird and then hooked under the free end and twisted upwards so that the leash passed round the thumb forms a 'D' shape over the leash running to the bird. The leash held between the first two fingers must not move.

4. The first two fingers are then brought round, anti-clockwise, to a point in front of the thumb.

5. The free end is then held against the inside of the thumb by the first finger which then eases a loop of free end through the loop 'D' (5b).

15c   15d

6. The thumb is then freed from the 'D' loop but retains its hold on the free end loop just created which is then pulled tight.

7. This should then form the knot, a single bow. This is tested by pulling with the left hand and if the knot holds the bird can be placed on its perch.

15e   15f

8. To finally secure the knot, the free end is passed through the bow and pulled, closing the bow onto the free end. This should not be pulled too tight.

This precaution is most important since a bird, more to pass the time than anything, will often play with its leash and/or jesses, and without this safety precaution has only to pull on the free end to release the knot.

15g   15h

9. When the bird is to be 'taken up' the free end is pulled back through the loop and the knot tested to make sure it still holds. The bird is then taken up on the fist and the free end pulled to release the knot. It is best if this is done by the left hand with the right hand holding the leash running to the knot. If the knot breaks prematurely the left hand is then free to quickly take up the bird without the leash being moved from hand to hand.

When a bird is to be tied to a screen perch the leash is

first halved and knotted in that position. The bird is then placed on the screen and the two ends of the leash passed in opposite directions round the perch top after which it is tied firmly to the perch with the swivel held in the centre of the top of the perch. The knot used to tie the bird must have no loops otherwise there is a risk of the bird, in a bate, getting a leg caught in the loop.

Whenever a bird is flown free, the leash and swivel are both always removed. Never, ever, under any circumstances is a bird flown free, as was done in the film 'Kes' with the swivel in place. No matter how well-trained a bird might be, there is always a risk that it will fly into a tree, and with its legs joined together by the swivel, there is a very real risk that it will get trapped on a branch. When they fly into trees, birds invariably make for the topmost branches where they cannot possibly be reached and freed.

Once a day, in the mews or some building with the doors closed, the jesses should be freed from the swivel and un-twisted, and at the same time checked for cracks. Any excess dirt or mud and droppings can be removed and, if desired, the jesse lightly greased with a good saddle soap or other preservative.

Many modern falconers advocate the use of the Aylmeri jesses invented by a former member of the British Falconers Club, Gus Aylmer. These consist of a simple leather band secured round the bird's leg by a brass rivet and having a slit beyond the rivet. A short leash with an end slit is then placed through this slit, and through its end slit the swivel is fitted.

Falconers have often complained that in a hunting bird the jesses trailing behind its legs are a hindrance and will serve to attract any wild falcons that might be in the vicinity. Should the bird escape, they may also cause it to become trapped and hang, even if there is no swivel in place.

Like most innovations, they have their disadvantages. Firstly, and I think most important of all, there is the prob-lem of fitting the 'short' leash into the jesse while the bird is standing unsecured on the fist. I maintain, and have always maintained, that a bird should be secured to the fist the moment it lands, and this is impossible with the Aylmeri. I am sure that there are far more 'lost' birds due to the Aylmeri than for any other reason, other than, possibly, breaks due to neglect of furniture in use.

The *HOOD* is the one piece of hawking furniture that nearly everyone can recognise and in this day and age it is of questionable value. Its function is to cover the bird's eyes so that it can't see, thus keeping it quiet and stopping it from trying to fly off the fist or perch. It was an essential item in the Middle Ages when birds were carried to and from the hunting-field on horseback, bumping and jolting carts or closely tied to other birds on the cadge. None of these conditions apply today when the only occasion a hood is needed is when more than one bird is being carried on a hunt, in which case the birds not to be flown at the next prey are hooded. It would be unfair to any bird to expect it to remain calmly on the glove or perch watching another bird hunting food.

> Harmless Lucretia, marking what he tells
> With trembling fear, as fowl hears falcon's bells.
>
> *Lucrece.*

The best way of describing the hood is to say that it is a cap of stiff leather that blindfolds the bird without touching the eyes. It must fit easily over the bird's head with the beak and nares (nostrils) protruding through an opening in the front. It is closed and opened by two pairs of leather braces at the back, one of which have buttons so that they can be easily identified.

Two types of hood are in common use, although there are several variations on the basic designs. The Dutch Hood is made from three pieces of leather and the Indian from only one. The Indian Hood is by far the lighter, but having only one set of straps is easily removed by the bird. The much heavier Dutch Hood is the more decorative

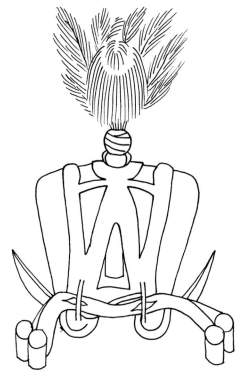

16   The Hood showing the 'braces'.

'traditional' hood usually featured in paintings and prints. Most commonly used hood today is the Anglo-Dutch which, as its name implies, is an amalgam of both main types.

The Rufter Hood was an 'emergency hood' usually only used on birds that had just been trapped.

For the Dutch Hood two pieces of leather are used for the sides and a third for the centre. Calf or pig skin are most commonly used the edges to be stitched being cut on the bevel so that the thread can be passed through the surface then out through the side, so that no trace of any stitching can be seen on the outside, which is often tooled or otherwise decorated.

Once the three pieces have been stitched the hood is placed on a block, soaked with water and moulded into shape. All joints are well boned and smoothed so that all stitches are pressed well into the leather and not left proud

17 A Hood.

leaving a rough surface. When dry the leather is polished and decorated and the inside lined with fine velvet so that there is no rough surface that can come into contact with the bird.

The much lighter Indian Hood does not need to be soaked and shaped over a block and, being much lighter and made of finer leather cannot be tooled and decorated.

Modern epoxy resins have now reached such a state of perfection that hoods can now be glued together rather than stitched.

Hoods are, from the bird's point of view, highly personalised items of furniture a separate hood being used for each bird. Also, it is not usually acceptable for a bird to have a working and 'best' hood, since the latter would probably never be worn enough to become acceptably comfortable to the bird.

In *North American Falconry and Hunting Hawks* by Frank Lyman Beebe and Harold Melvin Webster, of which the author has one of the original numbered editions, there is described a glued hood known as the H. J. Slijper's 'Canon' made from a single piece of leather and glued rather than stitched.

The instructions that follow outline how to make the pattern for a hood working from a single measurement on the bird in question. Drawing-up the pattern requires a fair degree of accuracy in geometrical drawing. The following instructions are based on those published by Beebe and Webster.

1. Draw a line *ab* with point *c* as its centre. *ac* is the basic measurement for the pattern being taken from a point just behind the bird's eyes and across the top of its head.

2. Point *d* is located so that *abd* is an equilateral triangle with *d* being located with centres at *a* and *b* and radius *ab*.

3. With centre at *c* and radius *ac* locate points *e* and *f* on line *ad* and *bd* so that *cef* is an equilateral triangle.

4. *ef* is extended to make line *gefh* parallel to *ab* so that *cag* and *cbh* are right angles and *ag* is parallel to *bh*.

5. With centre at *a* and radius *ac* locate *j* so that *agj* is a straight line. With centre at *b* repeat to locate *k*.

6. Extend *aj* to *m* and *bk* to *n* so that *mdn* is a straight line parallel to *ab*.

7. With centre at *a* and radius *af* make an arc above *cb*. With centre at *f* and radius *fa* make a second arc to intersect the first at point *o*.

8. Draw a line from *o* through *f* to point *p* on the base

line so that *op* is parallel to *cd*. Where this crosses *jk* is point *r*.

9. Draw a line *et* parallel to *rp* crossing *jr* at r_1.

10. With centre *g* and radius *gm* draw an arc through $r_1 t$ to *gh* to locate s_1 on *rt*. With centre *h* and radius *hn* repeat the process to locate point *s*. These arcs locate the beak hole.

11. With centre at *k* and radius *kc* draw an arc from *c* to a point *u* above and beyond *b*.

With centre at *j* and radius *jc* draw an arc from *c* to point *v* above and beyond *a*.

12. With centre *d* and radius *dc* draw an arc to cut *am* at *w* and *bn* at *x*.

13. With centre at *cd* where it intersects $s_1 s$ and radius to *r* draw arcs from *r* to cross *pn* at *y* and r_1 to cross *mt* and *z*.

14. With a slight curve join s_1 to *s*, *y* to *z*, *u* to *x* through *b* and *v* to *w* through *a*, *w* to *r* and *x* to *r*.

15. Complete pattern as illustrated on the drawing.

Should it be decided to make a hood to the pattern described then the pattern must be transferred to soft but light leather and *w* r_1 joined to r_1 *s* and *rx* to *ry*. If the hood is to be glued rather than sewn then the whole must be strengthened by gluing a small hem round the whole length of the bottom edge. If the hood is to be used great care must be taken to hone the inside to remove all rough spots.

A loop of leather or a group of chicken hackle feathers, well bound together, must then be firmly attached to the top of the hood. It is by holding the hood by this loop or group of feathers that the hood is fitted to or taken from the bird.

It is almost impossible to sketch or otherwise illustrate just how the braces used to open and close the hood are fitted. By pulling on one pair the hood is opened, and by pulling on the others it is closed. The system of interlacing the braces also serves to ensure that they are kept reasonably 'stiff' so that the hood will not slide open of its own accord.

Probably the best way to find out just how to fit the braces would be trial and error working from the illustrations provided or, better still, making your own drawing working from a hood that should be tracked down in the local museum.

Getting a bird to wear a hood requires training and hooding the bird itself is one of the falconers' arts that has to be taught, rather than be learnt from a book. A bird that is clumsily handled when hooded for the first few times will become 'hood shy' and always troublesome to hood. Anyone who has seen an expert hooding his falcon and then tried their hand will know exactly what is meant in the foregoing.

When a falcon is to be hooded it is taken on the fist in the normal way the hood being taken, by the plume, in the right hand, and brought towards the bird from below its eye level. The hood is held with the bottom angled towards the underside of the beak as it is brought upwards. As the hood gets close to the falcon's beak the bird will tend to lean backwards away from the hood, which is countered by a deft wrist movement, a twist of the wrist which in fact momentarily throws the bird off balance and forwards. At exactly the same moment as the bird is tipped forward the hood is slipped over its head with the beak coming through the opening. The bird is then lifted to mouth level so that one of the braces can be taken in the mouth and the other in the right hand, both are then pulled thus closing the hood.

To 'strike' or remove the hood, the braces are pulled by the teeth and right hand to open the hood and then with the hood held by the plumes in the right hand, the bird is thrown slightly backwards, while the hood is slipped forwards and off over the head. Good hooding is very much a question of timing and deftness learnt through practice under an expert's eye.

Many falconers or so-called falconers use the hood on all

their birds, falcons or not. This is totally wrong. Under normal conditions the hood should only be used on working falcons—and that does not include kestrels who should never be hooded, being too small to comfortably support the weight of a hood. Hawks and eagles should never, in this day and age, be hooded, except in very special conditions.

The author maintains that the hood should never be used on any bird, falcon or not, as a matter of form. It should only be used when necessary because the bird in question will not settle unless hooded. Proper and sufficient manning should eliminate the use for the hood. This attitude was first advocated to the author by the Secretary of the French Falconers' Club, Association Nationale des Fauconniers et Autoursiers Francais, a M. J. Francoise Terasse, in the mid-1950's when he was first elected to membership of that club while living in France.

Some birds, no matter how well manned they may be, will never settle to travel in a car or other form of mechanical transport. Such birds will have to be hooded when travelling. Also there are occasions in the hunting-field when the hood should be used. If more than one bird is with the hunting party then those not intended for flight on the next cast should be hooded. After all it is most unfair to expect a bird to stand quietly on this fist when in full hunting fettle and with quarry in plain view.

Hood my unmann'd blood, bating in my cheeks

Romeo & Juliet, Act iii, Sc. 2.

The *LURE*, as the name implies, is used to entice a bird back to the falconer when it has flown beyond the range of his voice or the sound of a whistle or when, for any one of a number of reasons, it has decided to remain comfortably perched in a tree. While eagles and hawks are usually trained to the fist, the falcon is normally also trained to the lure.

The lure most commonly used in this country is roughly

horse-shoe in shape, well padded and not infrequently weighted so that it is about three-quarters the bird's own weight. It is swung on a length of line which in some cases carries a weight of its own. To take up a falcon the bird is allowed to take the lure which is thrown into the air for the falcon to 'kill'. If the lure is too heavy then the bird can injure itself when it strikes and may also be forced down to land at too high a speed. Either instance could make the falcon wary of 'killing' the lure on future occasions.

The two 'wings' of the lure are sometimes decorated with Jay's wings or something equally colourful so that it is the more easily seen by the falcon. Various shapes and sizes of lure have been made from time to time, many having some most useful features for a particular purpose. At one point the Americans even went as far as designing a lure with wings that flapped.

> As falcon to the lure, away she flies.
>
> *Venus and Adonis.*

The most important item of equipment as far as the falconer himself is concerned is the glove or gauntlet. Made, preferably in buckskin, it is for the left hand only. For some of the larger birds with very powerful talons the parts of the gauntlet covering the back of the hand and the palm are quite often of double thickness leather.

As with jesses, etc., gloves are often advertised for sale in certain magazines, but any falconer worthy of his name should be able to make his or her own glove, thus obtaining a far better fit than if using an advertised glove.

Gloves should be made of soft, supple leather and sewn with well waxed thread, using the two needles as required for the saddle stitch.

CHAPTER FOUR

Training

Patience is the support of weakness;
Impatience is the ruin of strength.

Colton.

The book that can be used as a 'Do It Yourself' course in falconry simply cannot be written. It cannot be stressed too strongly that these notes must not be used as a guide to training by any would-be falconer whose only course is to contact an experienced falconer and see if he or she is prepared to take on a beginner. Secretaries of clubs, such as the Welsh Hawking Club, 63 Wenallt Road, Rhiwbina, Caerdydd, Wales, may be able to help.

Training a bird of prey, irrespective of its age, size and sex, is a lengthy process that requires both a great deal of patience and almost unlimited time. Some falconers and books tend to claim that various species of bird take a particular period of time to train, but far too much depends on the bird's nature and intelligence and the falconer's experience for such prognostications to be of any value. Obviously a bird that spends half an hour a day with the falconer will take far longer to train, if indeed it is ever trained, than the bird which is handled for three or four hours a day. Force cannot be used to train a bird, only patience and understanding, that understanding from which is developed the confidence that leads to man and bird becoming partners. They cannot work efficiently as master and servant.

In the Middle Ages a wild bird, especially the haggard,

was trained by a process known as 'Watching' or 'Waking' which in simple terms meant keeping the wild bird perched on the fist day and night until it took food from the falconer's hand without first trying to eat his fingers. This method of training is most graphically described in T. H. White's book *The Goshawk*. However, no thinking person could possibly claim that such a process served to 'tame' a bird. Keeping a bird awake and without food for long periods merely served to break rather than tame it.

> You must be watched ere you be made tame, must you?
> *Troilus and Cressida*, Act iii.

The only way to tame any bird or other wild animal is to gradually induce it to accept man as a friend; to realise that he can be trusted. To be successful man and bird must develop that very special sort of relationship that is born out of mutual trust and understanding.

In the Middle Ages that special relationship was probably not as important as it is today. Birds were very easily obtained and man as the falconer was only concerned with killing other animals for his food or for the thrill of the chase. If a bird he was training became too tame and trusting the falconer would probably have accused it of lacking fire and thrust. If he lost it because of a lack of trust he would simply trap and train a replacement. He argued that too tame a bird was useless as a hunter, although he respected and loved a proven hunter. The modern shepherd uses the same argument to defend his apparently callous treatment of his dog. It is an argument that is completely destroyed by the relationship between man and that hardest worked of all working dogs—the Guide Dog.

Apart from the possibility of 'hacking' the training of the eyass, passage and haggard birds, is the same save that the eyass needs far more flying to fully develop and strengthen its flying muscles. It was to develop these all important muscles that birds used to be hacked, which can really no longer be done in safety.

To be hacked a young bird is kept in the mews until it can fly from end to end and has lost its basic fear of the falconer. It will always have been fed at a set time and may even been observed getting restless as feeding-time approaches.

The bird is then allowed to leave the mews and fly free only returning to the mews when hungry and in need of food. However, before the bird is released the falconer tours the district appraising shopkeepers, farmers, police and so on, of his intentions and asking that a watch be kept on the bird so that he can be told as soon as it is seen seriously trying to kill its own food. Once the bird misses a meal, a sure sign that it has killed, or has been seen trying to kill, it is taken up for training. It is the need to know where the bird is living so that, if necessary it can be trapped, that makes the support of local residents so important.

Today, in spite of the law, there are still far too many so-called sportsmen who will shoot at anything that flies, not to mention those older gamekeepers who still maintain that the only good hawk is a dead one. An even greater danger comes from further afield. With most families owning cars there is a growing influx of weekend visitors to the country, many of whom have guns or cross-bows and who are only too anxious to prove their skill with their weapon.

The risks of hacking a bird are therefore now so great that very few falconers can risk giving their bird that really essential muscle developing period of freedom.

While a bird is settling down to being tied to a perch it is fed as much food as it will eat. Whenever possible the food is as close as possible to its natural diet, freshly killed animals. No bird should ever be fed live animals, this is both cruel and totally unnecessary. At this time, and whenever possible during training, many falconers try to feed their birds on the animals they hope to use them to hunt, so that when the time comes they will recognise them as food and hunt them more readily. Research carried out on wild birds has shown that the food fed to nestlings does have a bearing on the animals hunted when the birds are adult.

Quite often a freshly imported or taken bird will refuse food mainly because it fails to recognise the animal it is supposed to eat as food. When this happens all that is needed, more often than not, is to slit open the soft underbelly of the animal and expose its entrails. If that fails then it may eventually be necessary to force feed the bird, but not until the falconer has tried every subterfuge he can think of.

When dead animals are unobtainable then butchers meat must be used, only shin beef or stewing steak being acceptable. In no way can this diet be regarded as complete and roughage in the shape of meat on the carcase must be fed at least twice a week. Some organisations have claimed that roughage can be replaced by wrapping meat in cotton wool or some other substitute. Such a procedure can be fatal, as a post-mortem on a Kestrel once revealed. Its intestines were clogged with small threads of cotton wool.

A bird's beak is kept in trim by being worn to shape by cleaning meat off bones and so on while swallowing some bones and feathers, etc., often provides the bird with essential vitamins and trace elements, and although many of these can be found in supplements, there should be no doubt in anyone's mind that nothing artificial can replace the 'real thing'. Since nature has provided birds of prey with the ability to make pellets that are regurgitated after feeding that part of the bird's digestive system must be properly exercised if digestive disorders are to be avoided.

Once a bird is used to its block and has stopped leaping forward to the very limit of its leash every few minutes manning can begin. A bird must be tamed, or manned, so that it will stand quietly on the glove while the falconer carries it from place to place—even through the town.

The first stage of manning, and the hardest to complete, is getting the bird to stand on the glove. Some falconers do this by using food as bait, a procedure that could quite easily be carried out much later in the bird's training. As soon as an unmanned bird is approached it tries to get away

18 The head of a Lanner Falcon. Note the overgrown beak—
a hazard where captive raptors are concerned.

and starts pulling at the end of the leash with frantic leaps
forwards, an activity that can very easily lead to damaged
tail and wing feathers.

Probably the only way to lessen the risk of feather damage
is to get the bird onto the fist as quickly as possible. This is
probably best done by sliding the gloved hand deliberately
down the length of the leash until the swivel is reached
when the bird is lifted well clear of the ground and the free
hand used to lift it onto the glove. Once the bird is held on
the hand the leash can be untied from the perch.

It goes without saying that by far the best way to get a bird onto the glove would be to do so without it bating at all, but this is not always possible. All the same the falconer must always approach his bird slowly and steadily and do everything possible to avoid startling it and making it jump off its perch so that it has to be picked up off the ground.

Any falconer of any standing will make quite sure that when approaching an unmanned bird he does everything possible to try and avoid startling that bird so that it jumps off its perch. A very slow steady approach will often persuade the bird to stay on its perch until picked off and onto the glove, but when and if it bates, then the picking up should be done as quickly as possible but without undue haste which all too often leads to mistakes.

The bird that has been lifted off the ground by its leash will almost end up hanging by its jessies from which position it must be picked up and placed on the glove. This is done by placing the right hand palm uppermost, under the bird's belly with the little finger against the legs. The bird is then lifted very carefully onto the glove with the feet being lowered slowly and very gently indeed onto the glove.

By lowering the bird slowly onto the glove it is checked should it try to leap into a bate as soon as its feet touch 'ground', which nearly always happens with the unmanned bird. In this way the bird can be lowered very gently onto the glove and the risk of a bate lessened. Far too many falconers try and 'swing' a bated bird back onto the glove which has, on more than one occasion, led to damaged legs and leg muscles. Commonsense should tell any aspiring falconer that to swing a bird's whole weight against its legs is to ask for trouble.

The real manning begins with the bird standing on the glove and is designed to 'introduce' the bird to everyday life as seen from the fist. First, it has to learn to stand on the glove while it is carried and then while taken along quiet, then busy roads, and on into town, and so on. It is the introduction of the bird to everyday human life that is the real part of manning.

To begin with, while the bird will barely stand on the glove, let alone permit itself to be carried, manning classes are very short indeed, but at the same time as frequent as they are brief. By keeping the periods short, stress on the bird is kept to a minimum. Gradually, as the bird settles, the periods can become longer in duration but take place less frequently, with the ultimate aim of there being only one lesson per day.

The ideal timing would be to mann a bird for about one hour every morning, with the same period of time in the afternoon, while in the evening both man and bird will sit and watch television which, in all probability, will have a wonderfully soporific effect on both man and bird.

As soon as he can the falconer begins to feed the bird 'on the fist', the aim being to get the bird to associate the fist with food. To begin with the bird will obviously refuse to eat, but it can quite often be induced by stroking the beak or breast with a piece of meat, so that when the bird pecks at it in annoyance it learns that it is being teased by a piece of food.

As will prove to be the case with many phases of training, getting the bird to make that first step is by far the hardest part of the phase of training. Getting any bird to take that first piece of meat from the fingers can often be one of the most frustrating of exercises. Numerous ploys can be employed in this instance, the most successful usually being to stroke the bird's beak and breast with a small piece of meat, which should annoy it sufficiently to make it try and peck the offending object and so learn that it is really the meal it has been waiting for. Once the bird has begun to eat on the fist then all its food must be taken on the fist until training is complete—the bird must learn to associate being on the fist with food. Some falconers maintain that the bird should never even be picked up onto the fist without its reward in the shape of a piece of meat.

While learning to eat on the fist the bird must still be manned as much as possible—in other words the falconer spends as much time with his bird as possible. This must continue until the bird learns to accept with equinamity all facets of our everyday life.

Once he has manned his bird so that it can be taken any-where and not panic, the falconer takes the training a stage further. The bird must now learn to come to the glove for its food, the basic lesson of falconry.

Hitherto the bird has always been lifted onto the glove, now it must be induced to come there willingly. The glove, with a small piece of meat held between the finger and thumb is held just out of reach. The bird will lean forwards as far out from its perch as possible, but the meat must be just beyond its reach, only by stepping onto the glove can it eat. As the procedure is new, the bird will almost certainly be suspicious and therefore unwilling to co-operate so, if at the end of half an hour, it still has not stepped onto the glove then it should be left to its own devices, without the meat of course, for at least an hour, after which the falconer will try again for another half-hour or so.

A most important rule that must be remembered at all times is never, once the bird is reaching forwards, move the meat or the glove further away. The bird must, over a period of time, build up confidence in the glove containing its food and to move it away will only destroy any vestige of confidence it may have gained.

Throughout the rest of the day the falconer will keep returning to the bird for periods of between fifteen minutes and half an hour trying to induce it to step onto the glove for that same small piece of meat, the only food it will have been offered that day. If, by dusk, it still refuses to come to the glove then it is given about one-quarter of its normal daily rations and the battle rejoined about midday next day and so on, day after day until it will step onto the glove.

For stepping onto the glove that first time the bird is rewarded with a feast and allowed to gorge until it can eat no more. As a result it will be found, next day, that its weight has risen and that, not being hungry, it will not step onto the glove, so the process is begun all over again.

To begin with it will only have to step onto the glove once to be given fair rations, but very soon it will have to be made to step onto the glove for every single piece of meat that makes up its day's rations. It will soon learn to 'work' for all its food, so the simple step can be extended to a jump and then to a short fly and so on, the distance being increased at regular intervals.

If a bird is overweight it will be noticed that it is reluctant to work and that its interest in food increases as its weight drops therefore by recording his bird's weight, and the amount of food it eats, every day, the falconer will soon learn the exact weight at which his bird shows maximum interest in food, and equally important the amount of food needed to keep his bird at that weight and therefore in peak condition.

To begin with the hawk is asked to fly the length of its leash, after which it is worked on a length of nylon line known as a creance. The leash gives flights of two or three feet, but then on the creance the distance can be increased to six, twelve, twenty-four feet, then yards and so on.

Beginners must at all times guard against rushing any stage of training and this applies especially to flying on the creance. It is unwise to increase the distance any bird is being called, until the bird flies immediately it is called, at the existing distance.

Birds of prey are trained to work for their food and will only work if their weight is at the correct level. The danger is, as far as the beginner is concerned, letting the bird's weight get too low. All too often the assumption is that a bird that is proving reluctant to fly is overweight and in consequence the weight is reduced. The truth of the matter could be that the bird is a little uncertain, so the weight reduction has no effect. In fact the weight is reduced to a point where the bird really lacks the necessary energy and cannot fly. There is no rule that can be applied to ensure that a bird's weight is correct, such knowledge comes only from experience.

Some falconers can judge their bird's weight by feeling the flesh on either side of the keel bone. The flesh should be there but the bone itself should be quite sharp, with the flesh on either side to the point where the shape is no longer concave. The flesh must be there, firm but not flabby. A condition that can only be detected by experience not a written description.

The writer checks his bird's weight by bringing the bird to a point where, when it is still flying on the creance, it will fly readily for the first half of its daily ration, but shows a marked reluctance to fly for the second half, an indication that after the first half the bird no longer really needs food. For that second half it will probably still fly but only after it has had a good look round, even gone as far as having a preening session. The best possible check is to let the bird's weight keep on rising gradually and finding out at what weight it just refuses to work. The falconer then knows the top limit, the idea working weight will not be much lower.

A creance must be as light as possible, but at the same time strong enough to withstand the sudden stress caused by a bird, flying at full speed, suddenly coming to the end of the line. Nylon chords, such as those produced for picture hanging are, in the main, far too heavy to be used for a creance, nylon fishing-lines, which can be obtained in a variety of strengths, are probably the best available today.

The breaking strain of the line can be quite easily worked by taking the bird's weight then multiplying that by 30, 30 m.p.h. being about the top speed a bird will reach on a creance and then finally, for safety, doubling the final figure to give the required breaking strain of the creance for a particular bird.

When a bird is being flown on the creance, great care must be taken to ensure that there are no tufts of grass or weed on which the line can be caught up, thus stopping the bird's flight and bringing it down to earth short of the glove, which can very easily break its confidence in the falconer or the glove.

Usually a bird is flown from a gate or fence-post and soon gets used to flying from that spot. Then, when the time comes for it to be flown free, the falconer wonders why it is reluctant to come to his fist from a tree or other perch. He never thinks that the bird has learnt to associate flying to the fist for its food as working from a given point to the fist. Care must be taken therefore, to make sure that during the period during which a bird is being trained to the creance, the flying locations are changed regularly so that the bird does not get used to one particular perch or area. A bird must be taught to fly from off the ground just as much as from a perch, such as a gatepost or tree-top.

To call a bird some falconers use a whistle, some a call or shout, and others simply rely on the bird seeing the out-stretched glove. It is a matter of personal choice which method is used. A dog or police-whistle has the advantage that it can be used by a stand-in falconer should sickness or other absence require a bird to be flown or exercised by a stranger, but on the other hand it has the distinct disad-vantage of being hard to get at quickly in an emergency. A shout or mouth whistle does not have to be fished out of a pocket in an emegency but cannot be used by a stand-in. Personally the 'stand-in' who dares, or I should say, risks flying another man's bird is probably asking for trouble unless he is to have that bird in his care for a considerable period of time, in which case he will probably take it through a shortened period of training so that it gets to know and accept him before he tries to fly it free.

When the bird will fly, on the creance, for upwards of a hundred yards, from off the ground, out of a tree, or any other location the falconer might choose, the falconer must consider flying it free. He should have no qualms. If each stage of training has been carried out steadily and not been rushed he should have every confidence that the bird will come to him as soon as it is called. Only if he knows he has rushed things should he be unduly anxious.

The bird flying free, the period of training, if it is a hawk or eagle, is more or less over, and the bird ready for hunting. Most falconers will spend some time flying the bird free for exercise before entering it for its first hunt, probably a wise move, since it may give him or her an insight into the type of perch the bird will choose if given its own choice.

Even though a bird is to all intents and purposes trained and may even be hunting, the need for regular exercise still exists, in fact, it becomes even more important. If it is to be hunted effectively a bird must be absolutely fit and what athlete only trains at weekends?

It is this need for regular exercise that makes it impossible or unwise for many so-called falconers to take up the sport. The man who works from nine to five does not get home till after dark for a large part of the year and since it's also dark when he leaves for work he cannot exercise his bird regularly. Therefore, he should not have a bird.

Once trained to fly to the fist the falcon must also be trained to the lure, a process that follows similar lines to training to the fist.

When the bird is on its perch the lure, baited as always with a small piece of meat, is thrown onto the ground in front of the bird, which soon learns to jump onto the lure as soon as it lands. Next the lure is towed along the ground in front of the bird which then has to jump and land 'on' the lure to 'kill it', thus it learns that the lure has to be caught rather than landed-on like the fist.

Some falconers maintain that it is a good idea to train all birds of prey to the lure pulled along the ground. Even eagles will enjoy chasing a ground lure suitably baited, and should a bird ever prove reluctant to come to the glove it can often be taken-up from off a ground lure. Training a bird to the lure has been responsible for the taking-up of many a 'lost' hawk. The fattest of birds will often be unable to resist a dead rabbit towed along the ground, or even the leather lure suitably baited with a favourite titbit the bird has learnt to recognise.

When a falcon will readily chase a lure pulled along the ground it must learn to catch it, or foot it, off the ground. The lure is simply held at arms length and allowed to swing slightly a few inches off the ground and dropped the moment it is struck by the falcon.

Gradually the lure is made to swing higher and higher so that the falcon learns to catch well clear of the ground, while at the same time the distance the bird has to fly to the lure is being steadily increased. Before long the lure, as the bird closes, is thrown into the air where it has to be caught.

At this stage it will quite often be found that the falcon gets lazy and watches the 'flying' lure, and simply waits for it to land on the ground before pouncing on it and taking its reward. This must be stopped. One way is to throw the lure into the air almost vertically so that it can easily be caught on the way down, unless the falcon gets there first. By doing this the falcon is forced to catch the lure in the air or lose its reward.

As with every other stage of training, once the falcon has gained its confidence in a particular procedure, training is taken a stage further.

As the falcon approaches the lure is 'presented' or thrown towards it, but at the last moment swung back again so that although the bird has tried to 'foot', it misses. The first time this is done, the bird will fly on past the lure for a few feet, and then land and see the lure swinging gently just a few inches off the ground as it did during the early stages of training. The lure remains there swinging gently until taken after which the procedure is repeated.

It will not be long before the bird will give up landing when it misses; it will simply bank and turn back to take the lure. The next step is to make the lure harder to catch on that return trip, so that in the near future it is being made to miss twice before winning its reward by catching the lure.

Gradually the lure is made harder and harder to catch, and

the number of passes it has to make is steadily increased. To avoid the bird getting too used to a particular routine, the way in which the lure is swung and the number of times the bird has to pass it, varies so that every pass is in fact a genuine attempt to catch the lure, and not just a routine pass being made to make up the required number of passes needed to get at the meat. At the same time however, the number of passes made on most occasions is being steadily increased.

The lure is made progressively harder to catch while the number of passes that bird has to make is increased. Sometimes the lure is thrown high into the air for the kill, and sometimes it is pulled steadily away so that it can be caught. The idea is to make the bird work hard for every pass, never must it be able to anticipate what the falconer will do.

With a bird that is going to be hunted care must be taken to ensure that it does not spend too much time working to the lure before its first hunt, otherwise there is a risk that the bird will become 'lure bound' and only hunt the lure, ignoring real live game. Used properly the lure is the best way there is of exercising a bird and keeping it in peak physical condition.

A beginner should train himself to swing the lure long before he tries to swing it for one of his birds. A lure must be swung in a circular motion and then lunged towards the bird, checked, pulled back and the circular swinging continued, all without a break, and very smoothly. It can only be accomplished after quite a lot of practice.

The way in which a lure is both swung and then presented to the falcon is most important, if the bird is ever to be used for hunting; it must be done in a way that will make the bird 'kill' the lure in much the same way as it would kill its quarry. A good bird properly trained to the lure will hunt that lure with the same fire and style it reserves for its quarry.

Some falcons prefer to attack their quarry with a fairly short stoop and striking at the bottom, then climbing upwards on the over-run. Sometimes the strike is even made on the over-run.

High flying falcons, such as the Peregrine, are not always ideal birds for working to the lure. They stoop from such a great height that the lure cannot easily be swung in a timed arc large enough to give them time to make a stoop, so some falconers maintain that it is best not to allow these birds to reach too great a height.

The hawk's favourite line of flight when taking another bird, is from below the hawk making its over-run while still below the victim, and then waiting until the body falls to the ground before finally binding. When working a low-flying bird the upwards approach is not always possible, in which case the hawk will make whatever approach is possible.

Lures are swung on either short or long lines. For low-flying birds the 'long line' is preferable since, when the lure is presented, it can be kept swinging low much longer than with a short line. On the long line it is however, far harder to swing and keep moving smoothly. The short line lure is swung anti-clockwise and timed so that as the bird approaches it is swung forwards, checked and then swung smartly backwards which gives the bird a fraction of time when the lure is almost stationary, before starting the back-swing. If the lure is to be taken then that is when the bird has its chance, if it is not to be taken then the change to the back-swing must be very smooth and rapid.

The long line cannot be used for the hawk which has been trained from a stationary lure moved as the bird approaches. Such a bird has to be flown to a lure swung in a clock-wise direction, the lure being thrown up and beyond the falconer, but in front of the hawk. Later the lure is swung anticlockwise and thrown up in front of the falconer, giving the bird a far harder climb.

Two lines of approach for the falcon are shown from the vertical but the flight line for the lure, with the hands shown in the waiting position, is shown in the horizontal plane to illustrate how the lure passes in front of the falconer with the point of impact being slightly to one side, giving the bird a clear field of flight past the falconer.

It is not unusual for a falcon, once it has grown used to the lure, to start trying to carry it, which in some cases is

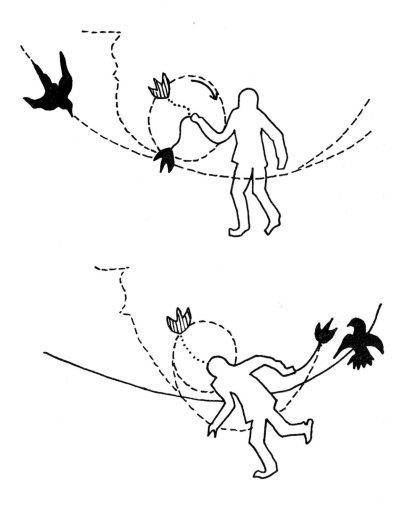

19 How the lure is swung showing the attack line of the falcon on the approach (top) and the pass (below) when the falconer has made the bird 'miss'.

quite natural, the bird being in the habit of carrying a kill to a favourite plucking-post. However, 'carrying' is a habit the falconer must break, since if allowed to develop the falcon will quite possibly 'carry' a kill away from the falconer.

Breaking a bird of the 'carrying' habit can be done in a number of ways, not least among which is making sure that the lure is never taken away from the bird once it has caught it until that bird has eaten its reward. In most cases falconers try to tempt the falcon away from the lure with a further reward. A further alternative is to increase the weight of the lure until it is too heavy for the bird to be able to carry it for any distance, but in doing this great care must be taken to ensure that the lure never gets too heavy. Falcons often really strike the lure and should that lure be too heavy or too solid, the bird itself will feel the impact and should this be too great, then the bird will soon become most reluctant to strike the lure in the air.

Some falconers increase the working weight of the lure by having a sliding weight which can run up the line to the lure, or remain on the other end of the line. Such a lure most certainly has its dangers, since any possibility of a weight swinging round attached to the lure must pose an element of risk to the bird, which can really only watch one thing at a time, and that will have to be the lure itself and not the weight swinging round on the other end.

In the Middle Ages, to encourage falcons to stoop at a high-flying or quarry lures, the falconer used lures that were quite often taken into the air by arrows. In this way they could be sent to heights that certainly could never have been reached by simply throwing or swinging by their line.

There appears however, to be no records by which we can learn just how this was done. I very much doubt if the procedure was entirely safe. Few people today can possibly credit that the arrow from the English longbow, famous for winning wars in France, carried more of a punch at short range than the .303 bullet used in the last war.

CHAPTER FIVE

Care of Sick and Injured, Conservation and the Law

We often say that the law is an ass, no more so than where birds of prey are concerned, at least that's how it appears.

For many years the law forbade the taking of native birds of prey, except under licence, but there were no restrictions on the importation of birds of prey. Eventually, under pressure from falconers, it was announced that the importation of birds would be controlled by licence, regulations that I objected to on the grounds that they would lead to the development of a black market.

To begin with the regulations were avoided by flying birds in through little known airports where customs officers were a little lax and then by bringing them in incrates that, according to the label contain poisonous snakes and which were, quite understandably not checked by customs!

As the regulations began to work and the various ways round them were blocked the growth in the illegal taking of birds from nests in this country accelerated. The media has, on more than one occasion, claimed that the Peregrine falcons are being sent out to the Middle East, in fact on *Pebble Mill* a spokesman for the R.S.P.B. once said that the Saudis weren't averse to saying that Peregrine falcons in the boot were essential ingredients in contracts for the sale of British buses.

That Society is completely out of touch and prone to making wild statements but that incident topped the bill of rubbish.

It is an offence to have in one's possession a recently taken bird unless that bird was taken under licence or is close rung, in other words has on one leg a sealed metal ring which can only be fitted while the birds are very young indeed. The system has far too many weaknesses.

In the first place it's quite easy to ring birds on their wild nests, take them at a later date and claim they were bred in captivity. It's even easier to take eggs, transport them in foam or under bantam hens and then complete incubation in an incubator again claiming captive breeding successes.

Legislation being considered during the latter half of 1981 is for the registration etc. of birds of prey in captivity. This will do little if anything to stop the thefts as already described but it will help create yet another Government department, employ a fresh army of Civil Servants none of whom know about birds of prey but who will no doubt effectively control falconry and the keeping of such birds of prey in captivity.

There is a need for the introduction of licences to possess birds of prey, something I have argued for for many years. Under such a scheme a licence granting committee would know that there are, for example, six pairs of Blue Nosed Falcons in captivity so that it would be reasonable to assume that this summer there would be six young falcons 'on the market'. They would therefore grant licences for four more persons to keep a Blue Nosed Falcon. The remaining two youngsters would be absorbed by those who already have licences but whose birds may have died or escaped.

In this way the market for illegal birds would be destroyed and if there is no market then the thefts will diminish. However when the Captive Hawks Report was published recommending such a course of action the Government, no doubt advised by clueless civil servants who couldn't see enough new jobs being created, rejected the proposals by arguing that possession licences would be arbitrary and too bureaucratic. What about that fact that licences are already needed to keep wild animals in captivity as well as smaller animals such as the Red Squirrel and Coypu.

At the moment applications for licences to take Golden Eagles into captivity are considered by the Scottish Advisory Committee, a committee supposed to be made up of experts. The majority of the members on that committee are appointed by the Secretary of State while others include representatives of the N.F.U., Landowners Associations etc., all of whom must know a lot about birds of prey. There isn't, on that committee, a single well known authority on birds of prey.

That the licensing scheme as operated at the moment doesn't work is possibly best illustrated by the fact that if you apply for a licence in advance the nest from which the bird is to be taken must be indicated. As if anyone knows in advance which nests will be in use the following season. Golden Eagles sometimes hatch two young birds but you can't get a licence to take a bird simply from a nest in which there are two youngsters, despite the fact that in less than one in fifty of such nests are the two young reared, the stronger nearly always kills the weaker. That little point is ignored, the interests of conservation aren't served by taking a bird that is destined to die into captivity in order to save its life.

The R.S.P.B. is supposed to be concerned with the protection of birds, but at the same time, despite its vast fund raising organisation it doesn't accept into care sick and injured birds. Such birds really do need help but they the Society ignores, it's more concerned with the establishment of more and more so called reserves into which it attracts more and more admission paying visitors who by their sheer weight of numbers frighten out of the area more and more birds and whose constant trampling damage fields and grasslands, often lands belonging to neighbouring farmers.

All over the country are small 'bird hospitals' financed by individuals which are for a very wide range of casualties whose work, which should really be done by the R.S.P.B. goes unrewarded and all too often unnoticed.

My eagles are used, during the summer months to give demonstrations before the public and during the winter months to illustrate lectures to schools. Never are they in fact used for hunting but the content of my lectures and the commentaries given to visitors to Leighton Hall where the demonstrations are given are always geared to stressing the need for conservation and the protection of Kestrels.

When the film *Kes* was first released I presented an item on *Blue Peter* condemning the film because it would encourage children to take Kestrels. Asked to contribute to the item the R.S.P.B., which should have been in the forefront, had 'No Comment'. Subsequently the film was shown many times on B.B.C. and the book studied by schools as one set for examinations.

It was organisations with which I'm concerned that pressured the B.B.C. to withdraw the film from screening and examination bodies to stop encouraging use of the book. Because Leighton Hall is known to have birds of prey in its care and because the R.S.P.B. just doesn't want to know about such casualties the Police and R.S.P.C.A. tend to call us in when casualties in need for care and attention are found.

Injured birds whose wings are so badly broken that they can't possibly be expected to survive in the wild need to be housed in aviaries for the rest of their lives, and aviaries for such birds cost at least £250 each to build. Such is the R.S.P.B.'s interest in conservation that it has gone to the trouble of writing to schools and or Education Authorities advising against the booking of the lecture we give on the history and practice of Hawking and which is used to publicise the need for funds to keep the injured birds in proper care.

The time has now unfortunately come where it would appear that the R.S.P.B.'s interest in the Protection of Birds extends only to those areas from which the Society can show a profit, necessary but expensive non income producing activities it ignores.

There are, in the British Isles today, far too many Societies and organisations devoted to the Conservation of this and that. Such organisations are too self-centred and stress only their own interests while ignoring others. The only organisations which truly consider the conservation of wildlife are the various County Naturalists Trusts. These organisations have in membership experts in all fields of conservation and study. They will look at all forms of life at the same time and not just the needs of a single facet. It is no use mounting guard over some rare birds when the guards themselves attract attention to another area in which there are some rare plants growing and which are then destroyed by the traffic.

Many of these Trusts run junior sections which provide first class facilities for youngsters and school groups, facilities that are more often than not devised by qualified teachers not well intentioned amateurs.

With nearly all sick and injured birds of prey the greatest enemy is shock; the shock of the accident itself and even worse the shock of being taken into captivity. Sitting-up with the bird, as happened in that case, will only have served to increase shock.

Any sick animal must be fed its natural diet, only rarely does a special diet devised by humans help. Milk and brandy were poison.

A weak animal that has not eaten for some time will also probably be dehydrated, so getting moisture into its system is the first essential. For birds of prey water on its own serves as a laxative and is therefore rather dangerous, but it has been proved that lukewarm water and oxo, or something similar, will often replace the missing moisture and at the same time provide a small amount of nourishment.

The bird should, therefore, have first been given water and an extract, secondly warmth, one of the best medicines for shock, and most important of all, peace and quiet, never the added trauma of constant human company peering at it.

Most young birds that are assumed to have fallen from the nest and are taken home for care, would have been better left where they were or, at the most, lifted back into a tree well out of the reach of cats and other marauding animals.

Birds that are hatched in trees must, at some stage make a first flight from one branch to another. If they miss their landing they can quite easily find themselves on the ground, very frightened and bewildered. They may well spend some time just standing where they landed wondering what to do next. Left to their own devices they will eventually fly onto a low branch or other easily reached perch, and from there up to another, until eventually they reach a suitable branch well off the ground. Such birds, quite obviously, do not need to be rescued and can easily be identified, because their wing and tail feathers will be fully grown, and there will probably only be a small amount of down on the head and possibly parts of the back.

Birds that are found on the ground still covered in down and without their wing and tail feathers, obviously need help. If possible they should be returned to the nest, but if this is not possible then they will have to be hand-reared. Food, as near as possible to their natural diet must be used, and that means other birds and animals. Mice can often be purchased from pet shops, who if they carry a reasonably large stock will, from time to time, be able to supply casualties. Mice brought in by the cat should not be used unless one is certain that no one living close by has been using any form of poison.

With very young birds the food will have to be cut into very small pieces and fed to the young bird piece by piece, a time-consuming process. As time passes larger pieces can be fed until the youngster is seen to start using its feet then whole bodies can then be fed. A careful study of a number of the more expensive bird books will give a good indication as to the food requirements of any wild bird.

Birds of prey, unlike sparrows and other much smaller

birds do not usually need feeding every hour or so, but all the same very young birds will require frequent feeding. A full, well-fed youngster will want to sleep for most of the day but as soon as it starts looking round and watching then it's getting near feeding time.

Only in exceptional circumstances should waif birds be fed on butcher's meat. Their digestions enables them to partially digest bits of fur, bone and feather regurgitating in pellet form those portions it cannot digest. Feeding butcher's meat does not 'exercise' that part of the bird's digestive system and were that to continue for any length of time, serious stomach upsets could result. Where butcher's meat is fed it should be supplemented with a multi-vitamin additive such as SA 37, obtained from and which must be used under the directions of the vet. It must not, however, be fed to young owls since there are indications that it can cause a deformity or death.

Fortunately raptors are hatched at a time when most poultry hatcheries are working at their maximum capacity, and most can be prevailed upon to part with a supply of casualties or culls free of charge and which can be deep frozen for a short time, but not more than two weeks but before being fed to any young bird they should be thawed out at normal room temperature for at least twelve hours.

Birds that are being hand reared should be housed on an imitation nest located at approximately eye level and handled only at feeding-time. Their quarters must be dry and warm and when the birds are very young the question of heating must be very carefully considered, especially at night time. Paraffin heaters must never be used under any circumstances. 'Black' pig lamps are quite satisfactory, but if these are unobtainable then the infra-red pig lamps will do equally well, although great care must be taken, no matter what heater is used, that the bird does not get too hot.

As a general rule birds of prey do not need to be given water, they obtain most of the moisture they need from their diet. In many cases water in any quantity is used as a laxative, so it cannot be given too often, if at all. If there is any doubt as to the bird's need for additional moisture, if one feels for example, that the meat is a little dry, the safest course to adopt is to dip the meat into the yolk of an egg.

20 Sick and injured birds can all too easily become tame and then tend to take over the house. This tawny owl, Emma, will never be able to fly again.

Once fully feathered, the future of the waif bird has to be very carefully considered. Every effort must be made to give it every opportunity to live a natural and free life—in other words, it must not be kept as a pet. However, young birds of prey learn how to hunt by watching their parents and then trying for themselves, but should they fail to kill their own food the parents will still be on hand to feed them and stop them from starving.

The waif bird that has been hand-reared must, however, learn how to hunt by a combintion of instinct and trial and error, and this takes much longer than when it has its parents to guide it. Some so called authorities argue that it cannot be done.

Many falconers hack birds back by flying them to a suitable post in an open area on which to find food. In this way they learn to recognize that post as being somewhere where, at a given time each day, they will find food. Since most birds of prey are instinctively independent creatures they will try to fend for themselves, and as they have more and more success will visit the hacking-post less and less. It can be argued that these birds are not really 'hacked back', they take themselves off in their own good time. Certainly man does not lose touch with them until they are really self-supporting.

This system has, however, its own rather special disadvantages which place a big question mark over its effectiveness.

A bird that has learnt or been encouraged to rely on man, can be said to lose its fear of him and will therefore become a danger to itself by being too trusting. Operators of bird hospitals can tell many gory tales of the fate that has befallen 'tame' kestrels, or of the trouble they have caused. Once such bird made its home on the window-ledge of a house where the lady had a phobia about birds. No one could encourage the bird to make its home elsewhere, it stayed, the lady had a nervous breakdown and her life was ruined.

A starving kestrel was taken to a bird hospital where it soon became obvious it had been reared by man. Not only was it tame, but it begged for food. It was soon back to its normal weight, but it escaped. The police, R.S.P.C.A. and press, etc., were all informed and its progress charted. The days passed, it seemed to be surviving so was probably fending for itself.

One afternoon it saw a lovely open field with short grass, just the place to look for mice. Pity about the men playing cricket though, they were probably scaring away all the food.

It flew towards the centre of the pitch aiming, as it had done so often in the past, when looking for food, to perch on a convenient head. It flew towards the batsman who, as it circled made a swipe with his bat, fortunately he missed. Unfortunately he did not miss the second time round.

He claimed the bird was attacking his face and going for his eyes. Every thinking person knows better, but who could prove otherwise? The real answer is that hacking must never be carried out in or near a built-up area, only somewhere where the nearest house is some distance away and the residents known.

An alternative to hacking by flying to the post, is to place the bird into a large aviary into which is placed live food that the bird can hunt. That way it has to learn to kill its own food.

No one can possibly like feeding a bird that way, but something of the nature has to be done. It, as a method, also poses legal problems from the cruelty point-of-view. It still does not solve the major problem however. The bird still sees that man is the provider of food, it only has to watch him put in the victims to see that. The only way that problem can be solved is to enclose the aviary completely so that all the bird can see is the sky. The sides are solid, it cannot see beyond its boundaries. Man feeds it through a special pophole so it can't possibly see him. In that way its dependence on him for food is broken.

One thing is certain. No one with any real consideration for birds of prey will ever, as was done on *Blue Peter* several years ago dream of simply letting a family of hand-reared owl go on the assumption that, since their feathers are fully developed and they can fly, they can also survive. Such a course of action is almost certain to condemn them to a slow death by starvation.

Broken wings and legs are the injuries most commonly met with and both require the services of a vet. Unfortunately not all members of the profession have any interest in or real experience with birds of prey. The honest ones will admit the fact and pass the bird on to a colleague. In most instances these injuries require the use of an x-ray machine, hardly ever is amputation required, so if it is recommended it is often a good idea to seek another opinion.

Where a wing is broken it can only be folded into the resting position against the body, care being taken to ensure that the break has been properly set, then the whole wing strapped to the body and immobilised for at least three weeks. The strapping must not interfere with the other wing which the bird will use for balance.

All too often vets who lack experience with birds suggest that a wing be amputated because the break is too bad to be properly set. Such drastic action is rarely necessary. A wing may well set in a bent position but unless the nerves are likely to be trapped, a wing in a bent position is more use than no wing at all. The removal of a wing disturbs, weight wise, the whole balance of the bird which will find it difficult to balance in the simplest of situations.

Wings cannot be put into splints or plaster but legs can. This is not something that should be done by the amateur, no matter how experienced. If the splint is too loose the break will not heal cleanly and the bird be in constant pain for a long time. On the other hand if the splint is too tight then the use will go from the foot and the leg die completely. I was once given a lovely Tawny Eagle that only had one leg because a well-known vet had put on a plaster too tight and killed the foot which came off with the plaster. That bird had to undergo several operations to trim back the bone, before we were able to get a respectable amount of flesh to fold over the stump to keep it clean and free from gangrene.

Generally speaking birds of prey are comparatively free from disease, but on the debit side often expire rapidly once struck.

Most of the more common ailments stem from some form of parasitical infestation. Birds that are fed a proportion of rabbit and other wild food should have their mutes regularly checked for worms, etc., about once in six months being the ideal frequency. Some falconers ignore this procedure by simply worming their birds at regular intervals, but such a procedure could quite easily lead to a resistance to the treatment storing up trouble for the future.

For a long time one of the major killers was 'frounce' which, unless caught in the very early stages is nearly always fatal. The onset can often be traced to pigeons and is due to a protozoan parasite, *Trichomonas gallinae*, first described by Rivolta in 1878. The disease is usually first apparent in the form of a cheesy-like growth on the tongue, with the bird possibly appearing to have some difficulty in swallowing due to the restricted use of the tongue. In its most virulent form the disease runs a fatal course in a week to ten days.

If frounce is even suspected the bird should be taken to a vet immediately. Never under any circumstances should a falconer try to treat his or her own bird when a disease that can spread as easily as frounce is suspected.

Equally lethal is Aspergillosis. In this case the culprit is a kind of mould *Aspergillus fumigatus* which can live, grow and sporulate, outside of living tissue. It is a fungal disease of the lungs and respiratory system that tends to strike hawks more than falcons. The early symptoms appear about a week before death, and are little more than apparently excessive tameness and a disinclination towards any form of exertion, with the birds tending to sit quietly with their feathers ruffled. They also begin to want to drink and there is, initially only a slight loss in weight. The end, however, comes with dramatic swiftness. Thirst increases and there is a complete loss of interest in food. If the bird is force-fed then anything taken is cast-up again within twenty minutes of being swallowed. Weight loss is obviously very rapid.

Cure is possible but prevention is far better. The disease

is usually caused by dust, keeping birds on a sawdust or sand-covered floor being one of the major causes. Floors should be hosed down and disinfected almost daily in hot weather. In winter quarters can be dried out quite easily using a fan heater.

Veterinary assistance is essential. One possible cure is an anti-fungicide known in America as Mycostatin while, also in America, Penguins, who often suffer from the disease, were treated with a fog machine misting the air with a solution containing Amphoteracin B.

Avian coccidiosis is another disease that infects birds of prey, and like the other two is highly infectious, running a swift and fatal course unless checked. It is caused by a microscopic single-celled animal known as coccidia and is transmitted from bird to bird by contact. The infecting animal has a complicated life cycle within the host and can form oocysts which can remain in the soil, still highly infectious, for several years. Any area that has held poultry or turkey, or building that has housed pigeons, must be held suspect.

As far as the falconer is concerned the disease gives some clear-cut symptoms and being well-known in poultry can usually be easily treated. First signs are flecks of red in the mutes, these being caused by inflammation of the intestines. A few days later the mutes turn watery and black and the castings will be a slimy dark brown and foul-smelling.

Later, it may be a day or two, or it could be a week, depending on the severity of the infection, the appetite will fail and any food eaten will be rejected; the bird will become very thirsty and sit sluffed up and listless with half-closed eyes until it finally falls off its perch and dies. There are numerous cures on the market with most vets who deal with poultry having their favourite. Ampro preparations have been used with considerable success in birds of prey.

Many captive birds of prey suffer from foot troubles such as Bumble Foot, corns or swellings on the foot, that are usually caused by the foot being in contact with a hard, smooth perch for too long. As a preventative perches should be changed regularly so that a bird is never on the same perch with the same foot grip for too long. The cure of bumble foot is a lengthy process and involves a long course of antibiotics rather than the surgery favoured by many vets.

A great many falconers who have behind them years of experience will often proudly proclaim that they are their own vets and do their own prescribing which may, up to a point be true, in that the vet will listen to them and then apply his knowledge to theirs. This does not mean, however, that the falconer should ever try and become his own vet, rather he should consult expert advice on every possible occasion. A phone call costs little and no vet will suggest taking a bird in for examination just to make money.

In many ways our lives today are governed by pendulums or waves. Today conservation is a pendulum in full swing. Twenty years or so ago it was a word we hardly ever heard, today it is grossly over used.

Conservation is really the preservation of both the animal and its environment but we live in an age when vociferous minorities, by their very persistence, often wield a power well beyond that warranted by their numbers.

Using conservation as a banner we find those who do not like predators and who would be quite happy to see all predatory birds and animals exterminated. Needless to say they refuse to consider the results of such a course of action.

Predatory birds and mammals kill to feed and in hunting naturally seek an easy meal. A sick animal is never very lively, so the sick are among the first victims. In this way the predator is a sort of doctor, by killing the afflicted it stops the spread of disease. They will also tend to kill more of those animals that are numerous and so they generally speaking help to keep the balance of populations by making sure that no one species becomes too numerous.

Therefore, predatory birds and mammals are necessary.

When a particular animal is in danger of extinction it has

quite often proved possible to save it by the reintroduction into the wild of captive bred specimens. Thus it can be proved that keeping animals captive can be of some benefit to Nature as a whole. The real falconer trains his bird and uses it for hunting, in other words he indulges in a blood sport, which may or may not be wrong depending on the readers' opinions.

He does, however, study his birds very carefully and for many years has been trying to breed his birds in captivity so that it will no longer be necessary to take birds for his purposes from the wild.

It is also a fact that, from time to time, every falconer loses a bird which probably goes wild. The Goshawk has always been the most popular rabbit hawking bird in this country and many birds have been lost over the years. Some of these have met up and are now breeding wild. Thus, although unintentionally, the falconer has reintroduced the Goshawk into this country.

For a number of years the majority of Goshawks used for hunting in this country were imported from Finland, where the bird is treated as vermin and shot on sight.

The R.S.P.B. is opposed to falconry, obviously that is only to be expected from an organisation dedicated to the protection of wild life, birds in particular. It has been rumoured that the society prevailed upon the Finnish Government to ban the export of Goshawks to the United Kingdom, which has in fact happened. If that is, in fact, the case, then the R.S.P.B. by their actions have condemned to death many thousands of Goshawks, some of which might have been saved by export to this country where they may well have escaped to help build up the natural population.

At the moment the falconer requires, from the Department of the Environment, a licence to take from the nest any native bird of prey. A licence is also required to import a bird of prey.

Unfortunately a licence is not required to keep a bird of prey, and the Protection of Birds Act of 1954 only makes it an offence to be in possession of a recently taken bird. Since anyone can appreciate that it must be very difficult for a court to determine just what is a recently taken bird there has, in recent years, developed a thriving black market in birds of prey. This would not have happened had the initial Act, drafted in the 1930's by the R.S.P.B. and amended almost annually since then, kept abreast of changing conditions and opinions.

The law, at the moment, requires that all birds bred in captivity be close rung, in other words, rung with a special ring within about twenty-fours of hatching, such ringing being recognised by the law as proof of captive breeding. Lack of any form of registering birds has meant that in recent years dealers have been in the habit of ringing wild birds, while still only nestlings and then when they are more or less fully grown taking them from the nest and selling them as captive bred birds, the law recognizing them as such.

In recent years the number of thefts of both young and eggs, of all types of bird of prey, have increased alarmingly. As far as the media is concerned falconry is to blame, which in many cases it probably is. However, a great many eggs are stolen by collectors who have no interest at all in the birds themselves. Falconry can in no way be blamed for those thefts.

When a single Peregrine, stolen illegally, can be sold for prices that almost certainly exceed £1,000 is it little wonder that the thriving black market continues to grow?

Some years ago reports were published that indicated the number of birds stolen each year. The last I saw claimed, if I remember correctly, that 73 per cent of the Peregrine nests in one region of Scotland were raided. Since that date I understand that no further reports have been published.

About three years ago, when I was writing an article on the theft of Peregrines, I contacted an old acquaintance who I knew carried out surveys on nesting Peregrines. To survey nesting birds he must have a licence since to disturb a nesting female can in itself be an offence. In no uncertain terms he told me that if he were to release any of his figures to me and therefore indirectly to the press, he would never be given another licence.

Why should the powers that be continue to be reluctant to release figures on the number of birds stolen annually?

There is really very little doubt that committees will continue to talk about changes in the law and it is just possible that within the next five years or so some real changes may be made.

Firstly, it must be made an offence to be in possession of any bird of prey that has not been acquired under licence, whether that bird is captive bred or not. Any applicant for such a licence shall be liable, before that licence is granted, to have the birds premises inspected to ensure that they are suitable for the bird or birds it is intended to keep. Anyone holding a licence shall also be liable to a spot inspection at any time while that licence is in force. The local police must be notified of all birds in the falconers possession and will have on file copies of all current licences. They too will be authorised to make, without a warrant, a search for birds not covered by the licence.

The fines for any infringement of the regulations shall be clearly laid down and, quite apart from any monetary considerations, shall include an automatic ban on the further keeping of birds of prey.

Such measures, which would be most unpopular with many so-called falconers, would not serve to stop illegal trading, but they would most certainly go a very long way towards stamping out a very nasty trade in lives.

A Government commissioned *Captive Hawks Report* published in 1981 does in fact recommend the introduction of 'possession licensing' but the Government has decided not to implement that recommendation because it is argued it would be too bureaucratic. Instead they will introduce a system of licensing and registration which will involve the employment of a small army of Civil Servants and cost Falconers a considerable sum of money every so often.

Glossary of Falconers' Terms

Accipiter A short-winged bird—a hawk. Identified by short, rounded wings, long tail and in the case of a true hawk, brilliant orange eyes. The scientific name of the bird includes the word Accipiter.

Arms The legs of a hawk from thigh to foot.

Austringer One who keeps and hunts accipiters as opposed to falcons. Rarely used today.

Bate, to The act of trying to fly off the glove when held by the jesses.

Beam feathers The primary wing feathers.

Bewit Short leather straps used to secure bells to a bird's legs.

Bind To seize and hold with the talons.

Block A smooth rounded block of wood used as a perch having in its centre a stake by which it is stuck into the ground.

Bowse, to To drink.

Bow perch A semi-circular perch usually having a padded centre. Derived from the habit of archers, who often doubled as falconers, of sticking their bows into the ground to be used as a perch.

Braces Leather straps, in sets of four, two of which have buttons, used to open and close hoods.

Brail A length of leather used to secure the wings of a bird having a slit in the middle. Still used by gamekeepers for pheasants.

Brancher A young raptor that has left the nest and which is still learning to fly and being fed by its parents.

Break into The act of breaking through the skin of a kill in order to eat—usually done through the soft underbelly.

Buteo	A bird of the buzzard family. Birds of this family are often called hawks by the Americans.
Cadge	A portable perch slung from the shoulders and used to carry a number of birds.
Calling off	The act of luring a hawk from an assistant at a distance.
Carry, to	To try and fly off with a kill or lure. The act of walking with a bird held on the fist.
Cast, a	Two birds flown or hunted together.
Cast, to	To release often by a gentle forwards throw, a bird. To act of disgorging a pellet of undigestible matter, fur, feather and bones, etc.
Castings	Pellets that have been cast.
Cere	The wax-like skin just above the beak.
Check, to	To change, in mid flight, from one quarry to another.
Cope, to	To trim a bird's beak and talons.
Come to	To begin obeying a falconer's call to the lure or fist.
Crab, to	When two birds, flying together, bind to one another.
Creance	A long length of light line on which a bird is flown during training.
Crines	The short hair-like feathers about the cere.
Crop, the	The Sack or Stomach in which food is stored before it is 'passed' or 'put down' into the stomach.
Crop, a	The amount of food eaten at a meal.
Deck feathers	The two central tail feathers.
Endew, to	To digest meat.
Ensayme **Enseame**	To purge a bird and rid it of superfluous fat.
Enter, to	To fly at live quarry for the first time.
Eyass	A young bird. A bird taken from the nest for training.
Eyrie	An eagle's nest.

Falcon A genus of birds sometimes called 'long wings', having long thinnish and tapering wings, a long middle toe and a distinct notch in the upper mandible. These birds have a scientific name beginning with the word 'Falco'.

Falcon, the The name often given to the female falcon.

Feak ⎫
Freak ⎭ The act of cleaning the beak with a stropping motion.

Foot, to To grab in or with the talons.

Frounce A disease of birds of prey, often fatal, which attacks the throat and tongue.

Get in, to To go up to a hawk after it has killed.

Gorge, to To eat a full crop of food.

Gorge, the The crop or first stomach.

Hack, to To give a young, or adult for that matter, the opportunity to learn to fly naturally while free.

Hack back The process of preparing and then releasing birds that have been injured or bred in captivity.

Haggard The adult bird of prey.

Haggard A term used to indicate the female adult.

Halsband A cord hung loosely across the back of an accipiter, ahead of the wings, and used to keep the bird's head down when it is thrown from the fist to give it a fast take off.

Hood A close-fitting leather cap or hat fitted over a bird's head and covering the eyes and secured by the braces.

Imping The act of repairing a broken feather by joining the two halves or replacing a lost half with a piece of feather from a previous moult.

Imping needle A piece of needle used to join the two halves of a feather. Originally a triangular rather than round needle made of iron that was dipped into brine before inserting into the feather. The growth of 'rust' acted as an adhesive.

Intermewed A bird that has moulted in captivity.

Jack A tiercel or male Merlin.

Jerkin	A tiercel or male Gyrfalcon.
Jesses	The leather straps, usually of buck skin attached one to each leg by which a bird of prey is kept captive.
Keen, to be	To be willing to work or hunt, to be sharp set.
Leash	The leather, now more frequently nylon, strap used to tie a bird to its perch.
Lure	An artificial prey used to lure or entice a bird back to the falconer.
Made, to be	A fully-trained bird is said to be 'made'.
Mail	The breast feathers.
Mail, to	To wrap up a bird for jessing or coping.
Make hawk	An old bird used to help train a young one.
Make in, to	To approach a bird that is on the ground with the intention of taking it up.
Mantle, to	To stand over a kill or food with wings outstretched and slightly forwards, tail spread and head lowered. A belligerent attitude.
Mews	The building in which birds are kept at night and in inclement weather. Traditionally the building in which they were moulted.
Musket	A male sparrowhawk.
Mutes	The excrement of birds of prey.
Nares	Nostrils.
Ostringer	An alternative spelling for austringer.
Pannel	A bird of prey's stomach.
Passage bird	A bird that has been trapped on migration—now more commonly used to denote a juvenile bird rather than an eyass.
Pelt	The body of a killed bird.
Penned, hard	Fully grown and developed feathers are 'hard penned'. Growing feathers are 'in blood'.
Petty singles	A hawk's toes/talons.
Pitch	The height to which a falcon rise and circles

Plume, to   To pluck, by another bird.

Pounces   A hawk's talons or claws.

Preening   Cleaning the feathers.

Preen gland   A gland at the base of the tail from which a bird obtains a secretion used to waterproof the feathers.

Principles   The two longest feathers on a bird's wing.

Pull, to   To eat while hooded.

Put in, to   For a quarry to dive into cover.

Put out   To drive quarry out from cover.

Put down   The act of passing food from the crop to the stomach.

Put over   Same as Put Down.

Quarry   Correctly the entrails of a victim of the hunt. Now more commonly used to denote a victim intended for the hunt or which has been hunted.

Rake away, to   To fly wide of the falconer.

Raking   Striking game or quarry in the air.

Rangle   Small stones given to birds to aid digestion by cleaning the crop. Now obsolete.

Ring up   To climb, circling, usually by a Merlin.

Robin   Male hobby.

Rouse, to   To raise the feathers and then have a shake.

Sails   Wings.

Seel, to   To sew the eyelids together instead of using a hood.

Serve   To put up quarry.

Sharp set, to be   To be in good hunting condition, keen, even anxious to hunt.

Slice, to   The act of discharging excrement.

Snite, to   To sneeze.

Stoop, to   To dive at quarry or the lure.

Strike, to— the hood   The act of taking off the hood.

Summed, full	To be completely moulted out.
Swivel	A swivel, two rings freely rotating used to join the jesses, the jesses are passed through one ring, the leash through the other.
Take up, to	To pick a bird from off the ground or off its perch.
Tassel	Male raptor.
Tiercel	Male raptor.
Tercel	Male raptor.
Tidbits	The small pieces of meat given to a bird as a reward. The forerunner of 'tit-bit' possibly.
Tirings, the	The indigestible parts of food, such as bones, fur, feathers, etc. fed to a bird.
Train	Tail.
Trussed, to be	To be seized in a bird's talons while still alive.
Unsummed, to be	To be moulting.
Varvels	Small brass plates fitted to the jesses and inscribed with the owner's name, etc.
Wake, to	To stay up all night with, in order to tame.
Wait on, to	To circle at a height waiting for food to 'take to the air'.
Weather, to	To place outside on a block or perch.
Weathering ground	Where birds are habitually put out in the daytime. Consists of a perch and some sort of shelter from wind and rain, etc., also quite often including a bath.
Warble, to	To stretch the wings above the head until they nearly touch. A good stretch.
Yarak, to be in	To be in keen condition, anxious to hunt. A bird must never be hunted unless in yarak. Not a traditionally British term.

FALCONAIDE

Exists to help conserve birds of prey and their environment and to raise funds for the development and operation of a

BIRD OF PREY HOSPITAL AND CONSERVATION CENTRE
AT LEIGHTON HALL, CARNFORTH, LANCS.

The Centre will look after birds like:

1. Emma, a Tawny Owl whose wing was so badly broken she can only walk round her aviary;
2. Pedro, a Little Owl whose wing had to be amputated after it was shot with an air rifle;
3. Nelson, who lost the sight of one eye after being hit by a car;
4. Fred, whose balance has been damaged after an airgun pellet grazed and cracked its skull;
5. Buzby, a buzzard with five shotgun pellets in its body where they can't be removed by a vet;

and many others who all need aviaries which cost over £250 each.

Medicine, heat and food can cost £5 a week per bird. Will you help?

Join FALCONAIDE or sponsor a fund raising event. Details from:

The Secretary,
Falconaide,
Slackwood Farmhouse,
Silverdale, Nr. Carnforth,
Lancs. LA5 0UF

Regular newsletters reporting all meetings.

Postal members voting and discussion facilities, etc.

PLEASE HELP US HELP BIRDS OF PREY